# RENEW YOUR YOUTH GOD'S WAY

JOHN BROOKFIELD

Copyright © 2020 John Brookfield

ALL RIGHTS RESERVED. This book contains material protected under International and Federal Copyright Laws and Treaties. Any unauthorized reprint or use of this material is prohibited. No part of this book may be reproduced or transmitted in any form or by any means, electronic or mechanical, including photocopying, recording, or by any information storage and retrieval system, without express written permission from the author/publisher.

Published by OS Press

ISBN: 978-1-64184-274-7 (Hardcover)

ISBN: 978-1-64184-265-5 (paperback)

ISBN: 978-1-64184-266-2 (ebook)

Cover and Interior design by JETLAUNCH

# TABLE OF CONTENTS

INTRODUCTION . . . . . . . . . . . . . . . . . . . . . . . . . . . . v

CHAPTER 1: LIKE THE EAGLES. . . . . . . . . . . . . . . . . . 1

CHAPTER 2: WHO SATISFIES YOUR
MOUTH WITH GOOD THINGS . . . . . . . . . . . . . . . . . . 7

CHAPTER 3: GOD'S WRITTEN
WORD/OUT YOUR MOUTH . . . . . . . . . . . . . . . . . . . 15

CHAPTER 4: THE POWER OF COMMUNION . . . . . . 21

CHAPTER 5: A MERRY HEART. . . . . . . . . . . . . . . . . . 25

CHAPTER 6: THE FIFTH GOOD THING
GOD PUTS IN OUR MOUTH. . . . . . . . . . . . . . . . . . . . 31

CHAPTER 7: HEALTH TO ALL YOUR FLESH . . . . . . . 43

CHAPTER 8: YOUR SLEEP WILL BE SWEET. . . . . . . . 53

CHAPTER 9: HEALTH TO THY BONES. . . . . . . . . . . . 59

CHAPTER 10: EARTHING. . . . . . . . . . . . . . . . . . . . . . 65

CHAPTER 11: BLESSED FEET. . . . . . . . . . . . . . . . . . . 71

CHAPTER 12: GIRD THY LOINS . . . . . . . . . . . . . . . . 81

CHAPTER 13: LONG LIFE AND
LENGTH OF DAYS ............................ 87

CHAPTER 14: WHAT RENEWING YOUR
YOUTH IS NOT ............................... 97

CHAPTER 15: IF YOUR EYE IS GOOD ............ 101

CHAPTER 16: SPIRITUAL POWER IN
THE PHYSICAL BODY ......................... 107

CHAPTER 17: THE YOUTHFUL SPIRIT .......... 117

CHAPTER 18: FLOOR SITTING/GROUND
SLEEPING ................................... 123

CHAPTER 19: YOUTH STEALERS ............... 131

CHAPTER 20: THE SUN SHALL NOT SMITE YOU .. 135

CHAPTER 21: THIRST NO MORE ............... 139

THE FINAL WORD ........................... 143

# INTRODUCTION

I strongly believe that this book, <u>Renew Your Youth God's Way,</u> will give you a new fresh revelation on how to truly renew and retain your strength and your youth physically, mentally, and spiritually. Quite often we hear the scripture in the book of Isaiah chapter 40 verse 31 quoted where the Lord says (But those who wait on the Lord, shall renew their strength; they shall mount up with wings like eagles. They shall run and not be weary; they shall walk and not faint.)

This verse has always fascinated me as I am sure it has fascinated many of you. As I began to seek the Lord, on how to truly renew my strength like the eagles, I can honestly say God began to give me strong revelation on this mighty blessing that we, as children of God, can truly experience.

Shortly after I began to seek God on this subject, he took me to Psalm 103. Psalm 103 actually lists the benefits that our Heavenly Father gives us as we make Jesus Lord and Savior of our lives. If you have never looked closely at these benefits before, I know you are going to get extremely excited. If you are familiar with these benefits listed in Psalm 103, I believe you are already starting to think about how the verse in Isaiah applies to these benefits listed in Psalm 103.

As born-again believers washed in the blood of Jesus, we need to know and understand the benefits that we have as children of God. Let's look at the first five verses in Psalm 103 that lists our benefits.

Psalm 103 – (NKJ) – (Bless the Lord, O my soul; and all that is within me, bless his holy name! Bless the Lord O my soul, and forget not all His benefits; who forgives all your iniquities, who heals all your diseases, who redeems your life from destruction, who crowns you with loving-kindness and tender mercies, who satisfies your mouth with good things, so that your youth is renewed like the eagles.)

Please take a moment to meditate closely on YOUR list of benefits that your Heavenly Father has given you. All of these benefits are a true blessing and belong to us as God's beloved children. We could easily spend a lot of time on each one of these benefits. However, the focus of this book is the last benefit listed where it says (So your youth is renewed like the eagles.)

In this book, I will show you the many, many things that God has clearly revealed in his written word and will show you how to renew and retain your youth physically, mentally, and spiritually, and the importance of doing so. You may ask if this could be God's answer to the Fountain of Youth? I believe you will find that it is and so much more as you read this book!

As we move to the first chapter, let's look again at the verse (So your youth is renewed like the eagles.) It is very interesting that God mentions the eagles, and it is also very interesting that the eagle is mentioned over thirty times in the Bible. We will focus our first chapter on the actual eagles, how they renew their youth, and how this applies to YOU!

I say you because this is a personal benefit God has given you if you are a follower of Jesus Christ. If you don't know Jesus yet, I strongly believe this book will put you onto the right path to finding him and you to will be able to walk in this powerful benefit!

# CHAPTER 1
## LIKE THE EAGLES

Psalm 103:5 (NKJ) (Who satisfies your mouth with good things, so that your youth is renewed like the eagles.)

As we focus on the verse above, let's look in particular at two key words that I want you to see and understand. I not only want you to see and understand these two key words but, I want them to literally penetrate into your very soul!

The first word is YOU! Yes, this benefit and this book was written for YOU so that YOU can have your youth renewed spiritually, mentally, and physically. This benefit and this book is so YOU can have life and life more abundantly.

John 10:10 (KJV) (The thief cometh not, but for to steal, and to kill and to destroy: I am come that they might have life and that they might have it more abundantly.)

The second key word that I want to penetrate into your soul is the word RENEW. The definition of the word renew is to restore, to revive, to replenish, to regain, to regenerate! This is very exciting as God says he has given YOU the benefit of renewing your youth like the eagles. Have you lost anything that you would like renewed or revived?

You might be thinking, well, I don't feel my best physically, or maybe you don't focus the way you used to. Maybe you are only sixteen years old, but you have lost your zeal and excitement for life. Maybe you don't sleep well as in the days of your youth. Maybe your back hurts and is stiff, unlike the days of your youth.

God wants to renew your mind, body, and spirit and I strongly believe as you read and apply these Biblical principles written in this book you will not only experience a mighty renewing but, you will also learn how to retain and keep this renewing no matter if you are sixteen years old or eighty-six years old. I believe you will experience a new lease on life and no matter your age or condition. I believe you will experience a renewing physically, mentally and spiritually with a great zeal for life and the kingdom of God. I believe that those around you will notice this new zeal and renewing as you soar higher and higher as God lifts you above any storm.

Exodus 19:4 (NIV) – (You yourselves have seen what I did to Egypt and how I carried you on eagle's wings and brought you to myself.)

You will experience this renewing of your strength in every way and mount up with wings like eagles!

Isaiah 40:31 (KJV) – (But they that wait upon the Lord shall renew their strength; they shall mount up with wings as eagles; they shall run and not be weary, and they shall walk and not faint.)

Please understand that it is God who lifts you up, and it is God who does the renewing. Just as the title of this book reads, it is not only God's will for you to renew your youth, but it is also time for YOU to renew your youth God's way!

Let's focus a bit on how the actual eagles renew their youth. As we focus on the actual eagle itself, it is interesting to know that there are about sixty species of eagles worldwide, and there are only two species in North America, which are the bald eagle and the golden eagle. The average eagle living in the wild usually lives to around thirty years old. However, there have been some eagles in captivity who have lived much longer.

It is also very interesting to know that the average eagle's eyesight is 4 to 8 times better than the average human's eyesight. The eagle can see 4-5 times farther than humans and is known to be able to, while in flight, spot a rabbit on the ground from two miles away. These facts can clearly show us where the term eagle eye comes from.

Eagles can also fly and soar at extremely high altitudes. The bald eagle, for example, is able to soar at altitudes up to 10,000 feet, which is just short of two miles high. Have you ever seen an eagle soaring in the sky? It is quite majestic, which I am sure is the reason that Agur said this in the book of Proverbs.

Proverbs 30:18-19 (NKJ) – (There are three things which are too wonderful for me, yes four, which I don't understand. The way of an eagle in the air, the way of a serpent on a rock, the way of a ship in the midst of the sea, and the way of a man with a virgin.)

To watch an eagle soar in the air without flapping its wings for a long time is mind-boggling. However, this is natural for the eagle because the soaring is one of the benefits that God gave it and created it to do. This is a very cool truth, however, just think for a moment, God created YOU for good works, and one of your benefits is renewed youth!

Ephesians 2:10 (NIV) – (For we are God's handiwork, created in Christ Jesus to do good works, which God prepared in advance for us to do.)

Job 33:25 (NKJ) – (His flesh shall be young like a child's; he shall return to the days of his youth.)

As we look to the actual eagles, we see that it goes through a process which is called molting. This molting process is not always clearly understood, and you can find differences in opinions on how the molting is done. However, to simplify the molting process, it is clear that the eagle sheds and rids itself of old feathers and replaces and replenishes itself with new feathers. In other words, the eagle gets rid of old baggage, which is weighing itself down and replaces it with new fresh feathers, which allows it to soar higher with better newly found vision just like the days of its youth.

Just as we learn to drop and rid ourselves of heavy old baggage that weighs us down, God can lift us up with newly found energy and vision. We can soar higher and higher above any storm with new energy and renewed youth spiritually, mentally, and physically! God grants us this ability to have new, better vision as we see things with clarity. You might ask, what is the baggage or things weighing us down? This baggage or old feathers can be a variety of things such as lack of forgiveness, envy, bitterness, anger, etc. These are things that Jesus died for on the cross for you. He bore them, so YOU don't have to, and as you let them go and go through the molting process, you can and WILL experience a new lease on life and renewed youth spiritually, mentally, and physically.

Like the eagles, you will soar high above the storm with a new zeal for life and a sharp, keen vision that will allow you to experience life and life more abundantly! Are you ready to experience life and life more abundantly and be zealous for the Lord as he renews your youth?

Elijah, the prophet in the book of Kings, was highly used by God, and Elijah had this to say in 1 Kings 19-14 (I have been very zealous for the Lord God almighty.)

I believe it was Elijah's zeal that enabled him to accomplish so much and be used so highly by the Lord.

Proverbs 23:17 (NKJ) – (But be zealous for the fear of the Lord all the day.)

You may say this sounds great, and I would like to have some of that zeal but, how do I obtain it? Well, as God renews your youth, this zeal and excitement will return in a mighty way. God will lift you up above your storm, and YOU will soar again as in the days of your youth.

As we move into the following chapters, I believe God will give you divine insight into the true power of his word and the never-ending love he has for YOU personally. I believe he will show and reveal to you why he created you and show you your personal destiny!

Psalm 139:16 (NKJ) – (Your eyes saw my substance, being yet unformed. And in your book they all were written, the days fashioned for me, when as yet there were none of them.)

# RENEW YOUR YOUTH GOD'S WAY

As God renews your youth, I believe you will sleep better at night and wake up energized with true purpose and a new spring in your step. I believe your outlook and vision will greatly improve as you will soar like the mighty eagles and become all that God created you to be. Let's move on to the following chapters and let God renew your youth his way!

Psalm 110:3 (KJV) – (Thy people shall be willing in the day of thy power, in the beauties of holiness from the womb of the morning; thou hast the dew of thy youth.)

# CHAPTER 2
## WHO SATISFIES YOUR MOUTH WITH GOOD THINGS

Psalm 103:5 (NKJ) – (Who satisfies your mouth with good things so that your youth is renewed like the eagles.)

In this chapter, we will look at the good things that God satisfies your mouth with, that cause our youth to be renewed like the eagles. I have greatly sought God on these good things, and I truly believe that he has given me a powerful revelation on what these good things are.

Even though each of these good things can be quite vast and can have many branches coming from them, I will share what God has revealed to me from his word about these good things. As we look at these good things, it is important to understand that all of these good things are benefits that our Heavenly Father has given us, and he tells us in his word not to forget his benefits that he gives his children.

Let's look at the five good things that God puts into our mouths so that our youth is renewed. The five good things are listed below.

1- Good Quality Food/Biblical Diet Principles.

2- God's Written Word/Spoken Out Of Our Mouth

3- Holy Communion

4- A Merry Heart/Joyful Spirit

5- Power of Tongues/Praying and Singing in the Spirit

As we move on in the following chapters, we will discuss and get revelation on each of these good things that God puts in our mouths. In this chapter, we will discuss the importance of good quality food or a Biblically-based diet. I will not get into great detail on a Biblically-based diet as there are quite a few books written in great detail on the subject of Biblical nutrition. Also, on the subject of proper diet and eating, God's word is quite straight forward. With this being said, no nutrition expert or dietician could ever show you a better way to eat for your health than the written word of God.

As my own personal testimony, I will tell you that with proper eating, my weight is now back down to 220lbs. which is the weight that I weighed when I graduated high school. I really never even tried to lose weight, I simply just started eating right and thanked God aloud that he was renewing my youth like the eagles in Jesus name Amen!

As I began doing this, it seemed like my weight just started to naturally drop. I will not, of course, guarantee you that you will lose weight after reading this book. However, as you apply God's principles of renewing your youth and understand this is your benefit, you can easily see how this can happen! Also, as you begin to experience more zeal and physical energy, you will become more active, which will naturally allow you to burn more calories.

Thinking about people in Biblical times, we can easily see that the majority of them were quite active, plus they were probably light eaters as well. A great deal of them were farmers and sheepherders, which kept them active and up on their feet most of the time doing manual labor.

Let's take a look at what God tells us to eat as we go back to the foundation in the very first chapter in Genesis.

Genesis 1:11-12 (NKJ) – (Then God said, let the earth bring forth grass, the herb that yields seed, and the fruit tree that yields fruit according to its kind, whose seed is in itself, on the earth; and it was so. And the earth brought forth grass, the herb that yields seed according to its kind and the tree that yields fruit, whose seed is in itself according to its kind, and God saw that it was good.)

As we look at this very first chapter of Genesis, in the beginning we see that God gave us the herbs and the fruit with its seed being within itself, meaning that the seed itself would cause it to reproduce. After that, as we read on in Genesis, we see that God created man in his own image and created male and female. As we read on, we see the great importance of the herbs that yield seed and the fruit that yields seed as he tells man this.

Genesis 1:29 (NKJ) – (And God said, see I have given you every herb that yields seed which is on the face of all the earth, and every tree whose fruit yields seed; to you, it shall be for food.)

Let's meditate for a moment as we get the simple but powerful revelation that God tells us in the very beginning, in the first chapter of Genesis, what he has given us to eat, and please notice the fact that God said it is GOOD!

I often think we read or hear a verse and don't take time to let it saturate our spirit, and we take it for granted, not seeing it with our spiritual eyes. Also, I want us to focus again on the fact that God tells us in the very first chapter of his all-powerful living word and he says that it is GOOD! What is good? What he has provided and chosen for us to eat is GOOD!

We have always heard men telling us that it is good for us to eat plenty of fruits and vegetables but, here we see God telling us that first. I personally have been trying to eat around ten to twelve servings of fruits and vegetables a day. Common sense also tells us that the quality of food is not the same now as it was back in Biblical days due to the quality of the soil and all the pesticides that are used today. For this reason I suggest if at all possible to try to eat organic fruits and vegetables.

Let's look at a verse in Psalm that also tells us the importance of eating vegetables that God has provided for us.

Psalm 104:14 (NKJ) – (And vegetation for the service of man, that he may bring forth food from the earth.)

As I mentioned before, I will not get into too much detail on what we are to eat but, I will give you a few more things regarding food that our Heavenly Father tells us about in his word. We see below that goats' milk is good for us as we read this verse in Proverbs.

Proverbs 27:27 (NKJ) – (You shall have enough goats' milk for your food, for the food of your household, and the nourishment of your maidservants.)

I have always heard and known that pure goat's milk is extremely nourishing, and now we know it by the written word of God in this verse.

We are told twice in the book of Isaiah that eating pig or swine flesh is not good for us.

Isaiah 65:4 (NKJ) – (Who sits among the graves and spends the night in the tombs; who eat swine's flesh and the broth of abominable things is in their vessels.)

Isaiah 66:17 (NKJ) – (Eating swine's flesh and the abomination and the mouse.)

I highly suggest that you read chapter 11 in the book of Leviticus. This chapter has 47 verses, which are entirely on what we should eat and should not eat regarding the animals, birds, and fish that God has created. This chapter alone could have a book written about it, so I highly suggest you read Leviticus chapter 11. Also, the chapter is pretty easy to follow and goes into great detail into what God says is good and bad for us to eat.

There are more and more people who are restraining from eating meat, poultry, and fish and have become strict vegetarians. There are, of course, different reasons for people becoming vegetarians, but it is clear that many do this simply because they feel eating animals is bad for them. However, God's word says clearly that he created cattle for man's food.

I will say that much of the meat and poultry today have growth hormones in it due to man giving the cattle and chickens these hormones to make them heavier and heavier. Because of this practice, I strongly suggest that you eat grass-fed beef and free-range poultry if at all possible.

As we have discussed the importance of eating good organic foods I will also mention that nuts are a great source of nutrition as well. I personally like pumpkin seeds and chia seeds, but I also enjoy walnuts and almonds.

Genesis 43:11 (NKJ) – (And their father Israel said to them. If it must be so, then do this; take some of the best fruits of the land in your vessels and carry down a present for the man – a little balm and a little honey, spices, and myrrh, pistachio nuts and almonds.)

I want to also mention the importance of staying properly hydrated and drinking good quality water. However, I will get into detail about this later in this book, in the chapter Thirst No More.

We all know that rich desserts are not good for us and especially the sugar that goes into them. I think eating sweets in moderation is okay but, we for sure need to stay away from them as a whole. However, it is important to understand that God's natural sugar is actually quite good for us and will not only give us energy but will also help satisfy our sweet tooth.

Proverbs 24:13 (NKJ) – (My son, eat honey because it is good and the honeycomb which is sweet to your taste.)

Yes, honey is God's natural sugar, and I like to take a tablespoon or two of raw honey at times right before a workout. You will also notice that raw honey does not raise your blood sugar levels like traditional sugar does.

The last point I will make in this chapter is an extremely important one and is quite often overlooked when it comes to eating and diet. This highly important point is eating in peace and quiet. Let's look at two verses below, which plainly tell us the importance of eating in a relaxed atmosphere without tension and strife.

Proverbs 17:1 (NKJ) – (Better is a dry morsel with quietness, than a house full of feasting with strife.)

Proverbs 15:17 (NKJ) – (Better is a dinner of herbs where love is, than a fatted calf with hatred.)

As you probably know our digestive system is of the utmost importance for the breaking down and absorbing of our food. The more that we are relaxed and in peace and take our time during our meals, the more effective our digestive system works which in turn enables us to process nutrients better, which equals better health.

As most of us know, our modern society seems to be always in a huge hurry and is stressed during meals. They have gotten away from taking their time and relaxing during mealtime. As we can see from the verses above that our Heavenly Father is telling us the importance of eating in peace and love instead of strife and hatred.

As we look at how God puts good things in our mouths and renews our youth, like the eagles, we see that one of these good things is good quality food that He has provided for us. And, to get the most out of these good-quality foods, we need to eat in peace. Remember how most families would all sit together and eat at the dinner table while they had fellowship? For the most part this has been lost due to everyone's busy, stressful schedule.

As I close this chapter let me say this. I highly encourage you to start taking a little more time to eat, and just as important, I encourage you to eat with a quiet peaceful spirit. Get into the habit of doing this and ask your Heavenly Father to help you get into this habit, for it is His will for you!

As we conclude this chapter remember to get into the habit of eating more high-quality fruits and vegetables for it is what God provided to you since the beginning. To drive this point home once more, we will close the chapter with the below verses from Daniel, and I encourage you to meditate on these verses and see the divine message your Heavenly Father is telling you! Even though there are multiple wisdom points in these verses, people often ask how long it takes to see a difference once they change their diet. Well, for the answer to this question, please look below, and I believe you will find the answer!

Daniel 1:12-15 (NKJ) – (Please test your servants for ten days and let them give us vegetables to eat and water to drink. Then let our appearance be examples before you and the appearance of the young men who ate the portion of the king's delicacies; and as you see fit, so deal with your servants, so he consented with them in this matter and tested them ten days. And at the end of the ten days, their features appeared better and fatter in flesh than all the young men who ate the portion of the king's delicacies.)

# CHAPTER 3
## GOD'S WRITTEN WORD/OUT YOUR MOUTH

## GOD'S WRITTEN WORD/THE POWER OF THE TONGUE

Proverbs 18:21 (NKJ) – (Death and life are in the power of the tongue, and those who love it will eat its fruit.)

Let's look closely and be sure that we understand this next section on one of the things God satisfies our mouth with so that our youth is renewed like the eagles. It is very evident that one of these things is actually the word of God, that is in our mouth, and when it is spoken, it brings life to us and those around us. God's spoken word is powerful, and everything is under its authority and must obey!

Hebrews 4:12 (NKJ) – (For the word of God is living and powerful and sharper than any two-edged sword, piercing even to the division of soul and spirit, and of joints and marrow, and is a discerner of the thoughts and intents of the heart.)

As we look at this verse in Hebrews, we can see that the word of God has great power, and we must learn to understand just how powerful God's spoken word is. We must also get in the habit of putting it in our mouth and speaking it! Speaking God's word aloud not only renews our youth like the eagles but, it as a major key to you moving into the true destiny God has called you to walk in. As we look at the verse in Proverbs again at the start of this section we see that death and life are in the power of the tongue or our words, and those who love it will eat its fruit. So as we look at this verse we need to understand that when we speak God's word aloud, we speak life to ourselves, those around us, and also circumstances around us and others. By speaking life out of our mouths it is important also to understand that we are speaking death to the things that are trying to hinder us from being who God has called us to be. I believe it is also extremely important to understand that the opposite can also work against us. In other words, when we are always speaking negative, toxic words we are speaking life to bad situations and death to the positive, so we must take heed to speak the truth and the positive, which is the word of God! Why do we need to speak the truth, which is God's word instead of the negative? To answer this question, let's look at what Jesus said in the book of Matthew.

Matthew 12:36-37 (NKJ) – (But I say to you that for every idle word men may speak, they will give account of it in the day of judgment. For by your words you will be justified, and by your words, you will be condemned.)

I strongly suggest that we look closely at this verse and meditate on it and let this powerful truth saturate our inner man. We must learn to put God's word in our mouth and keep it in our mouth, and God will renew our youth like the eagles. Someone may ask the question of why are words so important. Well, first of all, God tells us that they are and that alone puts this spiritual truth in motion for us to follow. However, let me tell you this, which will hopefully simplify my point and make you more conscious of the words that come out of your mouth. It is evident that the spiritual realm, even though invisible to our eyes is very active on planet earth. We understand that the angels of God are here to help us as his children but, we also need to understand that the unclean spirits of the devil are here to distract and hinder us from stepping into the destiny God has called us to.

This is why we must guard our mouths and only speak good positive words that bless and edify those around us and what can be better than God's written word coming out of our mouth. It is important to understand that the spirits on this earth have literally been around for thousands of years, and they do not sleep day or night. They have also had these thousands of years to study and observe man. I believe it is vitally important to understand that these spirits being either angels of the Lord or demons working for the devil. They hear our words and conversations and react to our words whether our words are positive or negative or life or death. This makes it vitally important that we speak God's word knowing that the angels of God hearken to his word when it comes out of our mouth. How do we know this?

Psalm 103:20 (NKJ) – (Bless the Lord, you His angels, who excel in strength, who do his word, heeding the voice of his word.)

We can clearly see in this verse above the angels of the Lord are listening for his word to be sent forth and heed his word to accomplish his word. On this planet earth, we are the voice of God, and when God's word is spoken out of our mouths his mighty angels heed these words out of his children's mouths. God's word out of our mouths gives life to any situation and death to the things of the devil. However, when we speak toxic negative words, it gives life to toxic negative things which are designed to hinder and stumble you. God tells us in Psalm 91 that he will give his angels charge over us to keep us in all our ways.

Psalm 91:11-12 (NKJ) – (For he shall give his angels charge over you, to keep you in all your ways, in their hands they shall bear you up, lest you dash your foot against a stone.)

As children of God, the angels are here to help us and lift us up from stumbling, and the more we speak the word of God, the more the angels hearken to it and will heed it. Let's look closely at these verses in Proverbs chapter 26, as I trust God will give us a powerful revelation in our spirit.

Proverbs 26:20–22 (NKJ) – (Where there is no wood, the fire goes out, and where there is no talebearer, strife ceases. As charcoal is to burning coals, and wood to fire, so is a contentious man to kindle strife. The words of a talebearer are like tasty trifles, and they go down into the inmost body.)

Here in Proverbs we can learn a powerful lesson about our words and how we must guard them and not speak toxic negative words. As God's word says here that where there is no wood the fire goes out. Point being, when there are no toxic negative words coming out of our mouths we are not fueling any fire or potential fire that can cause strife. If we use the wrong words which are not of God, we are fueling a negative fire which the devil wants to start and keep ablaze. As we read on we see that where there is no talebearer strife ceases.

So, when we speak positive Godly words, we are not giving place to the talebearer or the devil. So when we stop saying wrong things which are not of God strife will cease! Once again we are not giving any fuel to the fire, and by doing this, there will be no fuel. In fact, as we replace any toxic negative words we speak with positive Godly words we are giving fuel to the fire of God and the things of God into our lives. We need to add fuel to this fire, and set ablaze the things of God into our lives!

As we do this, we are putting good things into our mouths, and God renews our youth like the eagles! We also see in these verses in Proverbs that the words of a talebearer are like tasty trifles, and they go down to the inmost body. This shows again how powerful our words are and that toxic negative words can penetrate deep into us and others. It is important to understand that the word talebearer is used twice in these three verses and that the ultimate talebearer or liar is the devil who, in the book of John, Jesus himself calls him the father of lies. So we must put a guard over our mouths against negative words and speak only Godly, positive, edifying words of our Heavenly Father, which will also go down into the inmost part of our bodies as well as those around us as we speak blessings upon them. As God says, words will go down to the inmost parts of our bodies. Think of it this way. You would not want to ingest poison into yourself or have those around you ingest poison, so instead put good words in your mouth so that your youth and those around you can have their youth renewed like the eagles. As far as guarding our mouths against the talebearer, I love how David puts it in Psalm 142

Psalm 141:3 (NKJ) – (Set a guard, O Lord over my mouth; keep watch over the door of my lips.)

I have truly found that if we ask our Heavenly Father to set a guard over our mouth and to keep watch over the door of our lips, he will for sure, grant us our request.

# CHAPTER 4
## THE POWER OF COMMUNION

Luke 22:19-20 (MKJ) – (And he took bread, gave thanks and broke it and gave it to them, saying, this is my body which is given for you; do this in remembrance of me. Likewise, he also took the cup after supper, saying, this cup is the new covenant in my blood which is shed for you.)

In this chapter we will look at the power of communion and the importance it plays not only for the forgiveness of sins but also for your health and wellness that Jesus died for on the cross. Most often when people take communion they think about and focus on the shed blood which is for the forgiveness of sins. Of course the shedding of blood for the forgiveness of sins is vitally important, and without Christ's shedding blood we would not be able to go to heaven after our life here on earth. Along with Christ's shed blood we also have to accept this by faith and invite him into our hearts and ask Him to forgive us of our sins to go to heaven. If you have not asked Jesus to forgive you of your sins and made him Lord and Savior of your life, I highly encourage you to do this right now this very moment!

Along with the shedding of blood for the forgiveness of sins, Jesus also sacrificed his body which was bruised and broken for our healing, health, and wellness. So when we partake of communion and drink the wine or juice, it represents the blood shed by Jesus for the forgiveness of our sins. When we partake of the bread, it represents the broken body of Jesus, which is for our healing, health, and wellness. By his broken body and the stripes he received, we are healed.

Isaiah 53:4-5 (NKJ) – (Surely he has borne our griefs and carried our sorrows; yet we esteemed him stricken, smitten by God and afflicted. But he was wounded for our transgressions, he was bruised for our iniquities; the chastisement for our peace was upon him and by his stripes, we are healed.)

Peter 2:24 (NKJ) – (Who himself bore our sins in His own body on the tree, that we having died to sins, might live for righteousness – by whose stripes you were healed.)

It is evident that partaking of communion and understanding the difference between the juice for the blood that he shed and the bread for the broken body is crucial. When we understand this and partake of the bread, knowing by faith that as we take the bread, we are actually receiving the divine health and wholeness of Jesus, which helps us renew our youth, like the eagles, which this book is about. As it is written in Psalm.

Psalm 103:5 (NKJ) – (Who satisfies your mouth with good things, so that your youth is renewed like the eagles.)

Yes that's right. By understanding communion and taking of the bread by faith, you can be healed and to walk in divine health and wellness, which Jesus has already completed for you through his stripes on the cross! In this chapter, I believe God will give you strong revelation on the power of communion, and you will start to partake in communion and see your physical health flourish, as God renews your youth like the eagles. Let's look at what Paul wrote in the book of Corinthians showing how people took communion not understanding the power and benefits communion has.

1 Corinthians 11:28-30 (NKJ) – (But let a man examine himself and so let him eat of the bread and drink of the cup. For we who eats and drinks in an unworthy manner eats and drinks judgment to himself, not discerning the Lord's body. For this reason, many are weak and sick among you, and many sleep.)

As we look at the above scriptures we can see that Paul is saying once again that people partake in communion, not realizing the power and what it is designed to do for them, and why Jesus told us about it.

As we take communion we must understand the reason why, and we must also, by faith, understand that each time we partake of the bread we are not only becoming healthier, but it also helps us maintain our divine health through Jesus. As Paul said in Corinthians that many are weak and sick and even asleep, this means to die before their time simply because they do not understand or discern the Lord's body in the taking of communion. Because of Jesus on the cross we are redeemed from the curse of the law. The law, of course, has a wide array of sickness, degeneration, and the curse of quick aging and death before one's time. However, God wants us to know that through Jesus we are redeemed in every way, including divine health and healing, which we have been given through the power of the cross and the stripes Jesus suffered on our behalf.

I want you to know that it is time for you to walk in all of God's provisions, and the health of Jesus is one of those provisions. God says he has set a table before you and prepared it.

Psalm 23:5 (NKJ) – (You prepare a table before me in the presence of my enemies; you anoint my head with oil; my cup runs over.)

Yes! God has prepared a table for you and wants you to partake of his Holy Communion understanding, by faith, that every time you do, you receive the divine health of Jesus. You may be thinking right now, how often should I take communion? I suggest you take communion every day!

Acts 2:46 (NIV) – (every day they continued to meet together in the temple courts. They broke bread in their homes and ate together with glad and sincere hearts.)

Even though taking communion with your family or with a group of believers is great, it is also important to understand that you can also take communion by yourself which still has the same power and results. It is important to know that you do not need to have a certain type of wine or juice to drink for the blood nor do you need a particular type of bread to eat for the body. In fact, because you are doing this out of your faith, in the cross and in Jesus, you can simply drink water or any juice and use a cracker or a pinch of any kind of bread. Knowing this, let's look at how to actually take Holy Communion. Like I already said, you can take communion as much as you wish with my suggestion daily. As you take communion, I suggest taking it in a fashion that you know that you will become healthier and healthier every time you take it. Just as if you were taking a special supplement, you would know that the vitamin or supplement was helping you every time you took it. However, God's Holy Communion is so much more than any vitamin or supplement! Let's get started and look at how to partake of Holy Communion.

To partake, simply hold the bread in your hand and pray, Thanks Jesus for your broken body and the stripes that you bore for me on the cross. I know, and I declare that by your stripes I am completely healed from any sickness or symptom. I receive your divine health and wholeness in my body right now! (NOW EAT THE BREAD)

Now take the cup in your hand and pray; Thank you, Jesus, for your shed blood that has washed all my sins away. Your blood has made me righteous forever. As I drink I know that I receive healing, wholeness, and all of your benefits. (NOW DRINK)

You have just partaken of the body and blood of Jesus. Celebrate and give thanks as you can declare that the health and wholeness of Jesus is at work in your entire body right now, know that you have all the blessings Jesus has provided for you by the power of the cross!

# CHAPTER 5
## A MERRY HEART

Proverbs 17:22 (NKJ) – (A merry heart does good like medicine but, a broken spirit dries the bones.)

In this chapter, we will look at the power of laughter and having a merry heart. I have truly found that God renews our youth like the eagles, and as we develop a more joyous spirit, our heart truly does become merrier. I can honestly say that since God has renewed my youth physically, mentally, and spiritually I have noticed that I laugh and smile a whole lot more often. This seemed to just naturally occur as many other things began to happen. I remember, back as a child or even in my high school days that I laughed all the time and I had a merry heart. Then, as I grew older I still laughed some but, I seemed to laugh less and less. Now each day, I seem to laugh more and more, and I thank God for this because it is a true blessing, and I know now that this is because God has renewed my youth physically, mentally, and spiritually. You may ask how having a merry heart is a sign of renewed youth -- especially physically, mentally, and spiritually? This is a very good question to ask so, let's start with the physical aspect even though all three actually blend together, which I will reveal to you later. As your youth is renewed you will notice a more joyous merry heart, which I already mentioned. With this being said you will find it interesting that the average child laughs between 250 – 350 times per day. If you think about it, this is an amazing number since the average adult laughs about 12 times per day. You will also find it interesting that every time you laugh it boosts the immune system, reduces stress, and actually reduces pain in your physical body. Research has clearly proven all this in case you were wondering where I got this idea. So it is clear that the more we laugh, the better physical health we potentially walk in. There is an old saying that laughter truly is the best medicine. So please meditate closely on the scripture below that I just mentioned at the start of this chapter.

Proverbs 17:22 (NKJ) – (A merry heart does good like medicine but, a broken spirit dries the bones.)

I would like to highly encourage you to ask your Heavenly Father right now to give you a merry heart, and I know by faith in his word that your prayer request will be granted, and you will start experiencing the true blessing of having a merry heart. You may be thinking, well John I have a highly stressful life and it is hard for me to laugh and smile because of my circumstances. Well, I do understand the stresses of adult life. However, this is God's word, and once you stand on His word and thank Him for your merry heart you will start to notice a difference. Please remember everything starts with a seed and you may simply start to notice yourself laughing a little bit more each day. As this happens, you will start to reap the rewards and notice that you don't feel as stressed. From here, you will start to laugh and smile more and more, and truly develop a merry heart, and at the same time, you will begin to feel more energized and experience more joy in your life. Those around you will notice the difference and will ask you why you seem happier and more joyous. This will open up the door for you to tell them about Jesus and what he has done for you, and what he can and desires to do for them. As we mentioned, laughing and having a merry heart helps you physically as is strengthens your immune system, and is part of renewing your youth and your strength.

Laughing also renews your mind, as it is a part of renewing your youth like the eagles. Laughter reduces stress and makes your mind more relaxed and more at rest. As this happens, you are much more likely to hear the voice of your Heavenly Father. As your mind is renewed, you are at peace and at rest as this is God's will for you.

Isaiah 26:3 (NKJ) – (You will keep him in perfect peace, whose mind is stayed on you, because he trusts in you.)

With your mind being renewed and at rest, you are very open to the voice of God and able to walk in the destiny he has called you to walk in.

John 10:27 (NKJ) – (My sheep hear my voice and I know them and they follow me.)

As you can see a merry heart truly is a gift from God and part of his plan as he renews your youth physically, mentally, and spiritually. As you develop this merry heart you walk in joy and peace all day long, and see things differently as you have a cheerful countenance.

Proverbs 15:13 (NKJ) – (A merry heart makes a cheerful countenance.)

As you are renewed, your merry heart becomes a habit, and you are cheerful and joyous all the time, and you are excited about the things of God and fulfilling the destiny he has for you.

Proverbs 15:15 (NKJ) – (He who is of a merry heart has a continual feast.)

As you walk in this continual feast with a merry heart, you become very, very excited, and this excitement is seen by those around you, and they become more motivated and interested in the things of God as well. As God gives you a merry heart, you certainly become happier, more appreciative, and more trusting in the Lord.

Proverbs 16:20 (NKJ) – (Whoever trusts in the Lord, happy is he.)

I have personally noticed as God's children become renewed and develop a merry heart, they develop a more youthful younger-looking glow that can clearly be seen by others. That can attract attention to you, once again opening the door to the gospel. Part of this younger look, I believe, comes from the Holy Spirit inside of you as well as your physical health becomes better and more anointed because God's all-powerful word has been activated.

In this section, we have briefly looked at how a merry heart affects you physically and mentally, now let's touch on how it affects you spiritually. As you develop a merry heart, which is one of the traits of God renewing your youth, you develop much more zeal for the things of God which come from the Holy Spirit inside of you. You wake up in the morning not as tired but ready to start your day excited with how God has blessed you and anointed you, and you are ready to pass on some blessings to others. As you feel blessed and want to bless others, you truly walk with zeal for God all day long instead of thinking about yourself or being consumed with the things of the world that don't matter.

Proverbs 23:17 (NKJ) – (Do not let your heart envy sinners, but be zealous for the fear of the Lord all the day.)

You walk in a joyous fresh anointing, as God renews your youth, and your heart becomes merry. This fresh anointing bubbles over like a fountain because you know that God is with you, and you are blessed.

Psalm 92:10 (NKJ) – (But my horn you have exalted like a wild ox; I have been anointed with fresh oil.)

As you are anointed with this fresh oil, the Holy Spirit inside of you will direct your steps and your words, and you will begin to know that you are a true child of God as you are led by the spirit.

Romans 8:14 (NKJ) – (For as many as are led by the spirit of God, these are the sons of God.)

As you develop this merry heart knowing that God loves you and is with you and for you, you will know that you are being used by God to bless others, and you are victorious and will triumph because of your Heavenly Father's love and anointing on your life.

Psalm 92:4 (NKJ) – (For you Lord, have made me glad through Your work; I will triumph in the works of your hands.)

I have noticed a huge difference in myself in the mornings since God has renewed my youth and given me a merry heart. I have pretty much always been very sluggish in the mornings but, now I wake up much quicker and much more energized ready to start my day excited about what God has for me to do each day. I thank him for each day knowing that this is the day he has made and I will rejoice in it mightily.

Psalm 118:24 (NKJ) – (For this is the day that the Lord has made we will rejoice and be glad in it.)

As you start your day with this energy and excitement in the Lord, you will find that you are more obedient to the Lord throughout the day and that your energy and zeal will last through each day as you continue to rejoice in the Lord.

Proverbs 29:6 (NKJ) – (But the righteous sings and rejoices.)

I highly encourage you to thank your Heavenly Father, right now, for your merry heart and rejoice as you step out knowing that God is renewing your youth physically, mentally, and spiritually, and you will have a continual feast today, tomorrow and always for God has provided this for you.

Proverbs 15:15 (NKJ) – (He who has a merry heart has a continual feast.)

# CHAPTER 6
## THE FIFTH GOOD THING GOD PUTS IN OUR MOUTH

THE POWER OF TONGUES, PRAYING AND SINGING IN THE SPIRIT.

Ephesians 5:18-20 (NKJ) – (And do not be drunk with wine, in which is dissipation; but be filled with the spirit, speaking to one another in Psalm and hymns and spiritual songs, singing and making melody in your heart to the Lord, giving thanks always for all things to God the Father, in the name of our Lord Jesus Christ.)

As we look at the fifth and last good thing God satisfies our mouth with so that our youth is renewed like the eagles, I will say, in my opinion, this is the most important for those who are truly sold out for Jesus and truly desire to fulfill the destiny God has called them to walk in. Please understand that all five things are crucial, highly important to understand, and are the word of our Heavenly Father. However, my point here is this. I have found that being filled with the spirit and praying in tongues will make everything else work together and you will develop more revelation and understanding of God's word and the wisdom of God.

As God puts good things in our mouths, and as we know from the last section that speaking the word of God is one of the good things, we must understand that when the Holy Spirit speaks through us he is praying and saying the perfect prayer back to our Heavenly Father on our behalf. Often, we do not really know what to pray or how to pray to our Heavenly Father, but the spirit does. If we study the word of God, we know that we need to always thank him, and pray his promises back to him, but we do not always know or understand the circumstances behind what we are praying for. But, the Holy Spirit always does, and we can clearly see by this verse below that he will intercede on our behalf!

Romans 8:26-28 (NKJ) – (Likewise, the spirit also helps in our weaknesses. For we do not know what we should pray for as we ought, but the Spirit himself makes intercession for us with groaning's which cannot be uttered. Now he who searches the hearts knows what the mind of the spirit is because He makes intercession for the saints according to the will of God. And we know that all things work together for good to those who love God, to those who are called according to his purpose.)

As we pray in the spirit/tongues, we can rest assured that the Holy Spirit will intercede and pray the perfect prayer. This perfect prayer is God's will for our lives and our situation, which should give us tremendous assurance and allow us to rest in this powerful truth. I am convinced that the utterance of the Holy Spirit praying is the spirit praying God's written word back to him, and the written word the spirit is praying to the Father is the exact application of his word needed at the time for deliverance, healing, etc. I often start off simply praying in the spirit/tongues, and then I will suddenly start to sing in the spirit, and I continue to sing until I simply stop speaking in tongues. I truly believe that when the spirit goes from praying in tongues and then into singing, this is a sign of answered prayer and a breakthrough as the spirit rejoices by singing and giving Thanksgiving. I will tell you point-blank that I never sing, nor have I ever sung to myself, let alone in a group setting. However, I can sing for a long period of time in tongues, and I have learned for sure that the Holy Spirit singing is a definite sign of the spirit rejoicing on our behalf.

Proverbs 29:6 (NKJ) – (But the righteous sings and rejoices.)

I have also clearly found that as we pray and sing in tongues, this gives us a chance to rest physically and mentally, which we greatly need in this day and time. How do I know that praying in tongues allows us to rest and refresh ourselves? Let's look at these verses in the book of Isaiah.

Isaiah 28:11-12 (NKJ) – (For with stammering lips and another tongue he will speak to this people, to whom he said, this is the rest with which you may cause the weary to rest, and this is the refreshing; yet they would not hear.)

The praying in tongues truly allows us to rest and be refreshed and energized because our minds can be completely relaxed and quiet as the spirit prays. As you may know, many believers do not believe in praying in tongues, and you can see above in Isaiah that the Lord said many would not hear this powerful truth. If someone ever wondered if praying in tongues is important, we can look at a short verse in God's word that will, for sure, answer this question with a huge YES! Let's look at what the apostle Paul said in the book of Corinthians.

1 Corinthians 13:18 (NKJ) – (I thank my God I speak with tongues more than you all.)

As we look at this short, to the point, verse we see that Paul is emphasizing the great importance of speaking in tongues and being filled with the Holy Spirit. We must also remember that Paul wrote a large percentage of the New Testament. Paul makes it very clear in this chapter that he does not generally speak in tongues in church, but to himself which he does this to edify and build himself up. He prays in tongues a great deal to build himself up physically, mentally, and spiritually so that he can be a blessing to others and do the work God called him to do. We also know through God's word that praying in tongues is the best way to build ourselves up and to edify ourselves so that we can edify others, which is our calling. Let's look at this verse in Jude.

Jude 20 (NKJ) – (But you, beloved, building yourselves up on your most holy faith praying in the Holy Spirit.)

As we look at this verse, we can clearly see that if we wish to build ourselves up to the utmost, we must get into the habit of praying in tongues. Once again I want to say that this is how we need to build ourselves up so that we can truly be our best for the Lord and fulfill the destiny he has called us to walk in. As we look again at what Paul said – (I thank my God I speak in tongues more than you all.) – We see this tremendous tip or secret he revealed to us. Paul was truly a New Testament superstar, and he told us his secret to success in the Lord, which was being and staying built up and edified by praying in tongues. If the world's greatest athlete told you his secret to success, you would want to know; or, if the world's greatest businessman told you his secret to success in the business world, you would be all ears. Well, here was Paul's secret to success doing God's work for the kingdom, which was praying in tongues to build himself up, so that he could be a blessing to others. His time praying in tongues, which allows the Holy Spirit to speak, brought him closer and closer to God, which enabled him to hear God's voice and to do his will.

It is crucial that we are strong in the Lord first if we are going to be able to truly help others. I will give you an example of why we must prepare ourselves first if we are going to be able to help others. I am sure that many of you have flown on an airplane before and listened to the instructions that the flight crew gave. I am sure you remember them saying that if oxygen is needed you are to first put on your oxygen mask and then put on your child's mask. In some ways, this does not make sense, and one might think you should help your child first. However, if you think about this we will realize we must prepare ourselves first if we are truly going to be able to help those around us.

Proverbs 24:27 (NKJ) – (Prepare your outside work, make it fit for yourself in the field; and afterward build your house.)

As we draw closer and closer to God by yielding to the Holy Spirit inside us, we can truly start to walk with God and hear his promptings. We learn to do his will more and more each day, and we wake up refreshed and zealous for the things of the Lord all day long, knowing that our work will be fruitful.

Proverbs 23:17-18 (NKJ) – (Do not let your heart envy sinners, but be zealous for the fear of the Lord all the day; for surely there is a hereafter, and your hope will not be cut off.)

I can't overstress the importance of praying and singing in tongues, as it is a huge part of staying zealous for the things of God and having your youth renewed like the eagles. It will build us up spiritually but will also build us up physically by allowing us to rest, and it will also refresh us and energize us as it states in the book of Isaiah. We will truly feel closer to our Heavenly Father as this is his will for us, and he yearns to have a strong personal relationship with us. We will feel his everlasting presence more and more, as we will have a friend who sticks closer than a brother. I love the verse below, and we will look closely at the verse, as God will give us a powerful revelation into its meaning as we look with our spiritual eyes. I remember the day well when God gave me the revelation into its meaning.

Proverbs 18:24 (NKJ) – (A man who has friends must himself be friendly, but there is a friend who sticks closer than a brother.)

Let's look at this verse closely at what our Heavenly Father is telling us. We can see that we as believers have a friend that is closer than a brother, and he will stick with us during thick and thin. Think for a moment at what the word sticks actually means. If something truly sticks to you, it is there no matter what. No matter which way you turn, no matter where you go, no matter if you are walking, moving, sitting, or sleeping, it is stuck to you. It is stuck with you on your best day and stuck with you on your worst day. This is what our Heavenly Father is saying about our friend who sticks with us closer than a brother. This friend of ours who does this is the same spirit who raised Jesus from the dead, our best friend, the Holy Spirit. This is great news, to say the least. However, you might be thinking to yourself that you don't feel the friendship and closeness of the Holy Spirit at all. Or, if you do, you don't feel his presence all the time as if he was stuck to you or living inside you like the word of God says. If you are a born-again believer washed in the blood of Jesus Christ and don't feel the presence of the Holy Spirit, let's look at this verse again. I believe God will first show you why, and then how you can begin to feel his constant presence.

As we look at the verse we can easily see the Lord saying, there is a friend who can and will stick closer to us than a brother. However, as we look at the first part of the verse we see that a man who has friends must himself be friendly, or we might say, for a man to have friends he must first be friendly. Now as we look at the entire verse again, we can clearly see that the Lord is saying the Holy Spirit is with us and desires to be our best and close friend but, we must desire his friendship and be friendly with him first and then we will feel his constant presence, guidance, and leadership. The more friendly we are with him, the more friendly he will be with us, and the more he will help us and guide us.

The simple reason why we must first be friendly with him, to truly feel his presence, is that God gives us choices in everything we do. For example, for someone to be saved and receive salvation through the sacrifice Jesus made on the cross, they must make a choice to receive Jesus as their personal Savior and invite him into their heart and repent of their sins. The same thing works with accepting the presence of the Holy Spirit as your best and close friend; you must make a choice and first be friendly with him. Once you do this, you will have a friend who sticks closer than a brother.

We know through the word of God that to truly fulfill our destiny and make an impact on God's kingdom we must be friendly with the Holy Spirit. As we do this, we will learn to yield to him and let him lead us not only each day but throughout our entire lives.

Romans 8:14 (NKJ) – (For as many as are led by the spirit of God, these are the sons of God.)

As you yield and become led by the spirit, you will feel a huge difference. Not only will you feel more of a presence of God but, you will also feel more rested and energized physically and mentally as God puts good things in your mouth and renews your youth like the eagles. As you are friendly with the Holy Spirit, yielding and being led by him, you will find that the praying in tongues will be part of your daily life and that the praying and singing in tongues will not only be effortless but, also will be very relaxing and energizing. Let's look once again at what the prophet Isaiah said about speaking in tongues.

Isaiah 28:12 (NKJ) – (To whom he said, this is the rest with which you may cause the weary to rest, and this is the refreshing;)

With this being said, and since this book is written about how God renews our youth like the eagles, let me tell you a personal experience on how the speaking in tongues helped me not only be rested but also refreshed and energized.

My wife Sherry and I like to do a lot of hiking, and we greatly enjoy the more strenuous hikes that have a lot of hilly terrains. We have, for the last few years been going to the island of Kauai on vacation. We like Kauai, and we greatly enjoy the Na Pali Coast on the northwest side of the island where the Kalalau trail is. The trail starts on the Na Pali Coast where the road actually ends on a beach. This trail is about eleven and a half miles in length where it ends at a large beach. Most of the trail is very narrow, with a lot of rocks and roots protruding from the ground on the narrow path. The terrain is very hilly as the trail goes along the sea cliffs. The only way to get out is to turn back around and hike out the same way you came in. If you don't wish to hike the entire eleven-and-a-half-mile trail or you don't have time, you can simply hike in so many miles and then turn back around. Often, Sherry and I would be limited on time, so we would hike in several miles and turn around and hike out to get a good workout. There is also an eight-mile round-trip hike that starts at the beginning of the trail and then turns inward, going to a beautiful waterfall. The hike always seems to get very hot and humid going inward towards the falls because there is not much breeze in that area. No matter if we hike towards the inland falls, or along the sea cliffs, I always seem to sweat a lot due to carrying a plastic backpack on my back. And, of course, the nature of the hike causes you to put out a lot of physical exertion.

We carry a lot of water in the backpack I carry, and the little bit of extra weight does not bother me but, it is the hot plastic on my back, which seems to really heat me up over time. With this being said, I greatly enjoy hiking on the trail, and I find it to be a great workout going up and down the hills. After hours, or the whole day on the trail, I feel tired, and I always sweat out a lot of fluids. One morning, Sherry and I planned to spend most of the day out hiking the trail, so we planned to get up fairly early to get started. We got up that morning but, Sherry decided to stay back at the condo and just spend the day relaxing around the pool. When I heard she did not want to go hiking that day, this was a bit of bad news. However, the good news was she encouraged me to go by myself anyway. So I loaded my stuff into the car and started driving from our condo to the trail, which is about a thirty-minute drive. As I started to drive, I felt the strong prompting that God was telling me to pray in tongues on the entire hike all day long. I felt this so strongly I knew I had to be obedient and that he was, for sure, going to teach me something powerful.

Even though I planned to be obedient to what God was saying, I was thinking to myself that I have never even prayed in the spirit even close to the amount of time that the hike was going to be that day. However, I knew if God were telling me to do it, he would make the way! When I got to the end of the road where the trail starts, I could not find a place to park due to people going early to the beach. I had to park close to a mile back up the road and walk to where the trail started. As I parked my car and put my backpack on, which was loaded with bottles of water and some healthy snacks, I started walking down the road toward the trail.

As soon as I took the first step I felt like the Lord was telling me to start praying in the spirit, so I started to pray, and I also looked at my watch so I would know not only how long I was going to be hiking but, also how long I would be praying in tongues yielding to the Holy Spirit. As I started walking and praying I noticed that the sun was really bright, and there seemed to be a bit of humidity in the air that day, which is somewhat unusual for Kauai. I quickly marched along the road to the trailhead and began hiking up the steep trail, which is covered with large rocks for the first couple hundred yards. As I was climbing the rocks, I was praying in tongues while I was trying to move fairly quickly while still staying relaxed. After I was hiking for about the first twenty minutes or so I noticed my praying turned to singing in tongues, which pretty much remained singing throughout the rest of the day while I continued to hike the trail. I hiked four hours into the trail and four hours out that day while singing in tongues the entire time.

The only time I stopped was to drink water and to briefly have a quick snack. I seemed to sing in the spirit effortlessly the entire time, even though I never sing at all in my native English language. The singing was very relaxing as I hiked up and down the narrow path lined with rocks and roots. I could tell that I was moving faster than usual even though I was not really trying to push the pace. I also noticed that even though the humidity was higher than normal, I was not sweating as much as I normally do when I hike that route.

As I came off the trail, I walked back up the road to where my car was parked while still singing in tongues. I put my backpack in the car and started the engine, and as I did I looked at my watch and noticed that I had been praying and singing, in the spirit, for about eight and a half hours. I also noticed as I drove back to the condo that I felt very little fatigue, and I actually felt refreshed while I would normally feel quite tired after a day like that. As I recapped everything in my mind, it was clear to see that my hiking was faster than normal, I did not get near as hot as normal, I did not get nearly as tired as normal, and my body and mind stayed more relaxed during the entire hike. I also felt energized and refreshed afterward instead of simply feeling worn out and heat beat.

God really taught me something that day, which was, the closer we are to him, the less stress we feel physically and mentally, and when we pray in tongues we are yielding to the Holy

Spirit, our friend who sticks closer than a brother. When we do that, we can keep our minds and bodies much more relaxed even when we are doing physically strenuous endeavors. Our minds seem to be relaxed and in a state of bliss, so we don't feel near as much of the effort or stress as we would normally feel. Our hearts are in perfect peace.

Proverbs 14:30 (NKJ) – (A sound heart is life to the body.)

Once again, as Isaiah said, the speaking in tongues is the REST AND THE REFRESHING! It truly allows us to not only be in a state of rest but, at the same time, it refreshes and energizes us. As we yield to the Holy Spirit and speak in tongues, God puts good things in our mouths so that our youth is renewed like the eagles.

As we close out this chapter and section of praying in tongues, which is the fifth good thing God puts in your mouth to renew your youth, I want to highly encourage you to start praying in tongues if you do not already do so. It is something that our Heavenly Father has given us as his children. If we ask him in faith, he will freely give us his Holy Spirit and freely give us the ability to pray in tongues as we ask him and believe that we have received this ability! If you are uncomfortable about praying in tongues or unsure of its importance, let me encourage you again by what the apostle Paul said.

1 Corinthians 14:18 (NKJ) – (I thank my God I speak in tongues more than you all.)

Let's also look below at two more verses regarding the speaking in tongues.

Acts 19:5-6 (NKJ) – (When they heard this, they were baptized in the name of the Lord Jesus, and when Paul had laid hands on them, the Holy Spirit came upon them, and they spoke with tongues and prophesied.)

Mark 16:17 (NKJ) – (And these signs will follow those who believe; In my name they will cast out demons; they will speak with new tongues.)

Let's also look at what the apostle Peter said in the Book of Acts.

Acts 2:38 (NKJ) – (Then Peter said to them, repent, and let every one of you be baptized in the name of Jesus Christ for the remission of sins; and you shall receive the gift of the Holy Spirit.)

As we can clearly see in God's word that our Heavenly Father wants his children to be baptized with the Holy Spirit and be able to speak and pray with new tongues. This is clearly a gift, and to be quite truthful, we need to have this gift to fully step into the destiny God has called us into. Our Heavenly Father gives us good gifts, but like any gift, it must be received and used. Let's look at two more verses that tell us about the gifts that God freely gives us.

Matthew 7:11 (NKJ) – (If you then, being evil, know how to give good gifts to your children, how much more will your Father who is in heaven give good things to those who ask him.)

James 1:17 (NKJ) – (Every good gift and every perfect gift is from above, and comes down from the father of lights, with whom there is no variation or shadow of turning.)

As we read and meditate on these verses above, I know in my heart and by God's all-powerful written word that if you have not yet received the baptism and the gift of the Holy Spirit, it is your time, your day, your hour to do so! As God is talking to you right now, and I know he is, please prepare your heart and pray this prayer with me, and I know by faith you will receive the Holy Spirit right now. Remember this is the same spirit who raised Jesus from the dead and the same spirit who will stick closer to you than a brother all the days of your life!

PRAYER – Dear Heavenly Father I come to you in the name of Jesus, and right now, I ask you to baptize me with your Holy Spirit. By faith, I receive this gift from you, and ask you to help me yield to your Holy Spirit every day of my life as he leads me. I also thank you that I can now pray in tongues as the Holy Spirit gives me the utterance and intercedes for me. I thank you Father, in the name of Jesus!

Congratulations, you have just received the baptism of the Holy Spirit, and I encourage you to yield to Him and let him intercede for you as he gives the utterance. It is important to understand that the Spirit will never force you to pray in tongues, so if you feel funny words wanting to come out of your mouth, simply let them flow. The more you do, the more the words will flow and become fluent.

Proverbs 18:4 (NKJ) – (The words of a man's mouth are deep waters; the wellspring of wisdom is a flowing brook.)

You will soon greatly enjoy your new prayer language, and also feel closer to God and more able to understand the wisdom of God. Do not be concerned that the words coming out of your mouth are not of God but of the devil. I can assure you that when you ask God for this gift, he will protect you and that this gift comes from above. Also, if you are having trouble speaking in tongues, simply keep thanking God for the Holy Spirit, and it will happen as this is God's will and gift to his children!

This concludes these chapters on the good things God puts in your mouth so that your youth is renewed like the eagles. I highly encourage you to go back over these chapters again and start to implement these five good things into your life. As you do remember to thank God for renewing your youth like the eagles, for it is one of our benefits as a child of God!

IMPORTANT- Please reflect on this powerful thought. If you pray in the spirit for an hour daily for the next 24 years you have spent 1 full year praying in the spirit. Can you imagine how God will use this praying for you and his kingdom!!

# CHAPTER 7
## HEALTH TO ALL YOUR FLESH

Proverbs 4:22 (NKJ) – (For they are life to those who find them and health to all their flesh.) In this chapter, I will show you how to greatly tap into the benefit listed in the scripture above. Divine health and renewed strength and energy are a big part of having your youth renewed. You may not feel you have divine health, physical strength or energy at all. You may even feel you have lost these attributes. However, please notice the word renew!

Renew, of course, means to regain and to get again. Yes! God wants and desires you to renew and regain your youth, and this will happen if you follow his principles.

As I mentioned, it is your benefit, and the Lord tells you in his word not to forget this benefit!

Psalm 103:2 (NKJ) – (Bless the Lord O my soul and forget not all his benefits.)

In this chapter, I will reveal to you a truly amazing blessing that God taught me in his written word. This blessing is something you can implement right away. Yes, even today, which will not only enhance your physical health but also enhance every aspect of your life and those around you and help you step into your personal destiny that God has called you to!

This simple, but yet unique, principle was revealed to me a couple of years ago, when I began to diligently seek God on how I could become the strongest and healthiest possible for the cross-carrying ministry.

Proverbs 8:17 (NKJ) – (I love those who love me and those who diligently seek me will find me.)

The cross-carrying ministry I have been doing is where I physically carry, not wheel around, but carry a large wooden cross. I started carrying the cross on several roads and streets as a testimony to Jesus. The Lord made it clear to me to actually carry it instead of wheeling it around as a testimonial and to get people's attention.

People would often stop for prayer, or to thank me for my boldness for Jesus. They would also, at times, ask the weight of the cross and how old I was. When you see a sixty-year-old man physically carrying a large wooden cross weighing close to 200 lbs. for several miles, it gets people's attention.

This, of course, opens the door for me to share the gospel of Jesus with them. As I was seeking the Lord on how to be my physical best, to carry the cross for extremely long distances, he told me that good nutrition and physical training principles would help some.

However, saturating myself in his word is the secret and best way to reach and stay at my physical peak. The Lord also showed me that faith comes by hearing.

Romans 10:17 (NKJ) – (So then faith comes by hearing and hearing by the word of God.)

Please note it says faith comes by hearing not reading. Please understand it is important that you read God's all-powerful word. However, it is very easy to simply get into the habit of listening to God's word on tape, CD, or even on your phone. In fact, you can listen to the word of God for hours a day. You can listen to the word in the morning, getting ready for work while driving to work, or doing errands, or during the day, evening, or even have God's word playing softly at night in your bedroom.

Let me show you four basic principles that listening to God's word will do for you. The first, as I already mentioned, will drastically build your faith! Please also look closely at the verse below.

Proverbs 4:20 (NKJ) – (My son, give attention to my words; Incline your ear to my saying.)

The second blessing you will get is increased divine health. This chapter's name and opening scripture say, God's word is health to all your flesh. Not some of your flesh but, all of your flesh! I used the word saturate earlier, when it comes to God's word penetrating into your inmost being and parts.

How do I know this? Let's look closely and meditate on the verse below.

Hebrews 4:12 (NKJ) – (For the word of God is living and powerful and sharper than any two-edged sword, piercing even to the division of soul and spirit and of joints and marrow and is a disclaimer of the thoughts and intents of the heart.)

This verse is quite often quoted by pastors and teachers. However, they normally quote the first part of the verse. Let's look at the second part of the verse where we can see clearly that the word of God actually penetrates right into your joints and marrow. This is extremely exciting news because now we know that listening and playing God's word aloud actually affects our entire physical body. Yes, your joints, bones, marrow, your blood … everything.

Once again, as this chapter says, health to all your flesh! As we can now see in scripture, when you listen to God's word you are becoming healthier, stronger, and more energetic. I have for sure seen this myself as I have been listening and playing God's word daily. Here is something else I want you to understand. It is great to listen closely, as God's word is playing, and you will find yourself more and more wanting to listen to every word. However, even when you have the word playing softly, or you are not listening closely, it still penetrates into your physical body and is health to all your flesh and strength to your bones.

How does this happen? Because Hebrews says, the word of God pierces into your joints and marrow or your entire body.

The Lord says to incline your ear to his sayings, for they are LIFE to those who find them and health to all YOUR flesh! I strongly encourage you to read your Bible but also spent as much time listening as possible. For example, I hear all the time people saying they try to read a few devotions in the morning before work, but they find it hard with time and also being distracted by different things.

Try this as you get ready for work. As you shower and get ready in the bathroom, have God's word playing on your phone or CD. As you prepare and eat your breakfast, have it playing. As you drive to work, play his word. This will totally allow you quite a bit of Bible time first thing, and you will be building your faith, as faith comes by HEARING, and the word is PIERCING and PENETRATING into your entire body and creating HEALTH TO ALL YOUR FLESH!

I cannot even tell you how powerful it is to get into the habit of listening to God's word and how it will accelerate you into having your youth renewed. I will share a few simple ideas with you on how you can implement the hearing of God's word. You can get into the habit of playing the word in your house throughout the day. You can listen as you are doing yard work or housework.

Just like office buildings have soft music playing in the background, you can have God's word playing around you all the time. Just think how God's word will saturate your spirit and body as you get into this habit. If you know someone who is ill at home or in the hospital encourage them or their families to do this as the word of God has tremendous healing power!

Psalm 107:20 (NKJ) – (He sent his word and healed them and delivered them from their destructions.)

God's word has tremendous nourishing power to our entire mind, body, and spirit and the more we saturate ourselves in the word of God, the more we are nourished. Look at what Jesus said.

Matthew 4:4 (NIV) (Jesus answered, it is written; Man shall not live on bread alone, but on every word that comes from the mouth of God.)

It is extremely interesting what the verses below from the Book of Amos have to say about the word of God. Only in these verses, God is telling us what happens without the word of God nourishing us.

# RENEW YOUR YOUTH GOD'S WAY

Amos 8:11-13 (KJV) – (Behold, the days come, saith the Lord God, that I will send a famine in the land, not a famine of bread, nor a thirst for water, but of hearing the words of the Lord; and they shall wander from sea to sea and from the north even to the east, they shall run to and fro to seek the word of the Lord and shall not find it. In that day shall the fair virgins and the young men faint for thirst.)

As we look at these verses, we see that without the word of God, the fair maidens and even the young men will faint for the thirst of not being nourished by the word of God! Once again, we see the importance of saturating ourselves in the word of God which will renew our youth and strength physically, mentally, and spiritually.

As we start listening and continue to listen to God's word, we will saturate ourselves with his presence and truly be able to meditate on the Lord, his principles, and kingdom day and night. As we do this, what happens?

Psalm 1:2-3 (NKJ) – (But his delight is in the law of the Lord and in His law he meditates day and night. He shall be like a tree planted by the rivers of water that brings forth its fruit in season, whose leaf also shall not wither and whatever he does shall prosper.)

Notice that everything you do will prosper as you begin to meditate on his word day and night. One aspect of everything is, of course, your health. However, notice that your leaf will not wither which shows divine health as you are staying nourished and hydrated by the word of God!

Remember the verse in Amos where they grew faint from thirst because they did not have God's word to hydrate them. I can truly say, now since I have been listening to the word of God daily as much as possible, I have noticed that I am meditating on the Lord and his kingdom day and night. That's great; however, I am telling you this, so you too can begin experiencing this blessing, which will change your life. You will be able to step into all the benefits the Lord has for you, as you continue to saturate yourself in his word. Your path and vision will become brighter and brighter.

Proverbs 4:18 (NKJ) – (The path of the just is like the shining sun, that shines ever brighter unto the perfect day.)

Learning and applying the word of God is truly the key to all blessings and to stepping into your personal destiny and the Promised Land. Look at these verses in Deuteronomy and see how they apply to learning and meditating upon the word of God and moving into your destiny.

Deuteronomy 6:6-11 (KJV) (And these words, which I command thee this day, shall be in thine heart; And thou shalt teach them diligently unto thy children and shall talk of them when thou sittest in thine house and when thou walkest by the way and when thou liest down and when thou risest up. Thou shalt bind them for a sign upon thine hand, and they shall be as frontlets between thine eyes. Thou shalt write them upon the posts of thy house and on thy gates. It shall be, when the Lord thy God shall have brought thee into the land which he swore unto thy fathers, to Abraham, to Isaac, and to Jacob, to give thee great and goodly cities which thou buildest not and houses full of all good things, which thou fillest not and wells digged which thou diggest not, vineyards and olive trees, which thou plantest not; when thou shalt have eaten and be full.)

Once again, the word of God is the key to renewing your youth as well as all of God's blessings, protection, and provision! In this day and time, where we have all types of distractions coming from modern technology, we can also use this technology to our advantage for God's kingdom by saturating our mind, body, and spirit with the word of God.

One simple way is to listen daily as much as possible, which will enable us to truly meditate on God's word day and night. By doing this, we will be able to truly write God's word on the tablet of our hearts!

Proverbs 7:3 (NKJ) – (Bind them on your fingers; Write them on the tablet of your heart.)

Proverbs 3:3 (NKJ) – (Let not mercy and truth forsake you; Bind them around your neck, write them on the tablet of your heart.)

Another point I would like to make about listening to God's word and his word being health to all your flesh is this. You can also have the word of God playing at night softly in your room as you sleep. Not so loud that you can't sleep but quietly in the background as you sleep. My point is this. As we have learned from Hebrews 4:12, God's word pierces right into your spirit and body even when you are not listening closely. The average person spends about one-third of their life sleeping, so why not make use of this time and let God's word go into your body, and spirit like an IV would go into you with a constant drip.

I strongly believe that having the word on at night in your bedroom or house will greatly enhance your health and help write God's word on the tablet of your heart! Imagine the effect this can have on a baby or small child as the word saturates them. You may say their mind would not understand; however, their spirit is totally developed, and God's word will go into their spirit and body.

(As it is written, the word of God is sharper than a two-edged sword and pierces even to the division of soul, spirit, joints, and marrow.)

I encourage you to play the word of God softly at night, and by doing this you are looking to Him and giving Him your best and a place.

Psalm 63:6 (NIV) – (On my bed I remember you; I think of you through the watches of the night.)

Psalm 132:4-5 (NKJ) -(I will not give sleep to my eyes or slumber to my eyelids; Until I find a place for the Lord.)

Playing his word softly at night is, for sure, giving a place to the Lord! I am sure this will also help you sleep soundly, which brings me to the third blessing of listening consistently to God's word.

The angels of God come and hearken to his word. His word playing puts you in the presence of God and creates a heavenly atmosphere in your home, and you learn to abide and dwell in his presence.

Psalm 103:20 (NKJ) – (Bless the Lord, you His angels, who excel in strength who do his word. Heeding the voice of his word.)

Psalm 91:11 (NKJ) – (For he shall give his angels charge over you, to keep you in all your ways.)

Psalm 91:1 (NKJ) – (He who dwells in the secret place of the highest shall abide under the shadow of the almighty.)

As you play aloud and listen to God's word, you greatly grow in the Lord and continue to dwell and abide in the presence of Jesus! By doing this, you will also drive away and keep the devil and unclean spirits at bay. They cannot stand the word of God and the presence of the Lord. How do we know this? Let's look at the perfect example that Jesus himself taught us.

While in the desert, Jesus started being tempted by the devil, and Jesus continued to stay, it is written and he used the word of the Father against the devil. Jesus did not have the angels remove the devil or punch him in the nose, but instead Jesus used and spoke the written word of God. After Jesus spoke, the scripture tells us this.

Matthew 4:11 (NIV) – (Then the devil left him, and the angels came and attended him.)

Once again, this shows how powerful the word is. When you are listening aloud to the word, the word is being spoken out of the mouth of the speaker, and death and life are in these words of God.

Proverbs 18:21 (NKJ) – (Death and life are in the power of the tongue.)

So as these words of God are being spoken, they are life to you and health to all your flesh, and the things of God, and death to all the bad things. This is extremely exciting, and I hope this encourages you to start to play God's word consistently. Let's briefly recap the four huge blessings you will receive from listening to the word of God!

1- Your faith will greatly increase as faith comes by hearing the word of God.

2- God's word is health to all your flesh and strength to your bones.

3- Listening to the word will bring you into the presence of God and help you dwell there.

4- The word of God brings life to the things of God and death to the unclean things.

IMPORTANT – Please reflect on this powerful truth for a moment. If you listen or have God's word playing around you for 2 hours a day for the next 24 years you have listened and let God's word soak into your spirit and physical body for a total of 2 years. Can you imagine what that will do for you and those around you!!

# CHAPTER 8
## YOUR SLEEP WILL BE SWEET

Proverbs 3:24 (KJV) – (When you lie down, you will not be afraid; yes you will lie down and your sleep will be sweet.)

Sweet sleep is a blessing from God and also a promise to his children. In this chapter, I believe you will receive a powerful revelation from your Heavenly Father on his PROMISE of sweet sleep and the importance of sweet sleep. First of all I will say that sleep and proper rest are important parts of having your youth renewed like the eagles.

As God renews your youth it becomes easier and easier to walk in the blessings of sweet sleep. As you probably know millions of people have difficulty sleeping because of a wide variety of reasons. We will not take the time to specifically get into a wide variety of reasons. But, we will look at the reasons of fear and anxiety, which I believe is safe to say that pretty much everything else springboards off of. The reason I know this is because that scientific research has shown that restlessness at night normally does come from fear and worry; fear and worry about different things, no matter if the person is fearful of the dark, or the night itself, or if they lie awake worried and anxious about what happened that day, or if they are concerned about the next day's events.

Even though I believe this research, but more importantly God's all-powerful written word clearly reveals this to us. Let's look closely at the verse in Proverbs first that we started the chapter with. The first part of the verse states that when you lie down, you will not be afraid. God clearly is showing us here that this is the main reason, and the thing his children encounter that makes them struggle with the sweet sleep, he has already provided and promised.

He goes on to say that, yes, you will lie down and your sleep shall be sweet. We can see that when we are not afraid, worried or anxious, our sleep WILL be sweet. Let's also look at a verse in Psalm that tells us pretty much the same thing as God reveals to us the problem which tries to rob us of our promised sweet sleep.

Psalm 4:8 (NKJ) – (I will both lie down in peace and sleep; for you alone O Lord, make me dwell in safety.)

Let's look at this verse above closely as well. God tells us as we lie down we will both be in peace and sleep. This is telling us again when we are at peace we will sleep. Why will we be at peace and sleep? The reason is as we look to the rest of this verse. God says, because of Him alone He makes us dwell in safety! It is very clear as we look at the verse in Proverbs and this verse in Psalm that God is showing us that what can rob or steal our sleep is fear and anxiety. We know that Jesus came to give us life and life more abundantly and that the enemy is here to kill, steal, and destroy. Let's look at this scripture as we see this truth.

John 10:10 (NKJ) – (The thief does not come except to steal and to kill and to destroy. I have come that they may have life and that they may have it more abundantly.)

As we can see in this verse that our enemy, the devil, comes to steal, kill, and destroy. With that being said, we know that anything that tries to steal our peace and sleep comes from the devil, not of God. Because Jesus came to give us life more abundantly. So if you lie down to sleep and you feel fear, worry, anger or anything that is attempting to steal your peace, you know that it comes from the devil trying to rob you not only of your peace but also of the sweet sleep God has promised you when you are at peace.

Let's look at this scripture below that tells us to be at peace when the sun goes down, and not to be angry because this will allow the thief, the devil, to steal our peace.

Ephesians 4:26-27 (NKJ) – (Be angry and do not let the sun go down on your wrath, nor give place to the devil.)

We see here that anger when we lay down, gives a place to the devil and gives him an open door to steal our peace and sleep. Why is our sleep so important you may ask? Let's look at the two main reasons. First of all, as you probably already know, the average person spends about one-third of their life sleeping. The second reason is that our sleep and getting a good night's rest is vital to us living a productive life, serving the Lord and fulfilling the destiny God has called us to walk in.

Who knows this other than us? Well our enemy the devil knows this, and that is why he wants us to be in fear, angry, worried, etc. when we lie down because it can rob us of the sweet sleep that God has promised us. As we look briefly at the first reason that our sleep is so important is that it consumes one-third of our life, and I have found that during this time of sleep we can actually make huge gains spiritually. When we lie down in peace and sleep while trusting in God and meditating on his word and ways, we will drift off to sleep, giving the Holy Spirit inside us an open door to minister to us during our sleep.

I am sure that many of you reading this book have woke up in the night to go to the bathroom, with a Bible verse in your head, or a Christian song playing in your heart, or God may even be giving you a special word.

Also, think as you awaken in the morning how you will get up out of bed refreshed, with a word from God or a song or verse in your thoughts. The reason for this is because you gave a place to God as you lay down to sleep, and the Holy Spirit was ministering to you and having fellowship with you.

Let's look at these verses in God's word that show how the word of God and the Holy Spirit minister to us as we sleep, when we give a place to him, and meditate on his word as we lie down.

When you put him first and bind God's word upon your heart, you are promised this!

Proverbs 6:22 (NKJ) – (When you roam they will lead you, when you sleep, they will keep you; when you awake, they will speak with you.)

This verse in Proverbs has become so true and powerful in my life since I have been meditating on God's word and praying as I fall asleep. I always wake up with scripture in my mind or a Christian song in my heart, or sometimes simply praising God and feeling his presence more. I have noticed this being so strong since God has renewed my youth like the eagles and my trust in God has become simpler and more childlike. Just as a child trusts and looks to his father and mother in such a simple trusting way, God also wants you to trust him in this way, and this will happen as your youth is renewed.

You become more mature in the Lord, who gives you this youthful trusting spirit. Look below at this short, simple verse that shows how God is with you as you sleep and how you can feel his powerful presence as you give a place to him as you lie down.

Psalm 139:18 (NKJ) – (When I awake, I am still with you.)

I remember when I was a child, and my natural father came into my room when I had an earache. He put his hand on my ear as I went to sleep. I remember that to this day; it was extremely comforting. I fell asleep and remember, when I woke up later, he was still in my room sitting in the chair right next to my bed. I remember as a child how comforting this was and how our Heavenly Father watches over us as we sleep. He is always there, but it is up to us as to how much we can feel his presence. By feeling his presence and trusting him and resting upon him is what takes away our fears and anxieties and gives us the sweet sleep he desires for us.

Psalm 34:4 (NKJ) (I sought the Lord and he heard me, and delivered me from all my fears.)

As we seek him, he delivers us from all our fears; so, I encourage you to seek him, meditate on him and give a place to him as you lie down, which will give you sweet sleep as you feel his presence. Let's look below at this verse, which once again shows the vital importance of giving a place to him as you lie down at night.

Psalm 132:3-5 (NKJ) – (Surely I will not go into the chamber of my house, or go up to the comfort of my bed; I will not give sleep to my eyes, or slumber to my eyelids until I find a place for the Lord. A dwelling place for the mighty one of Jacob.)

As we give a place to our Heavenly Father and meditate on his word before we fall asleep, our fears and anxieties will melt away, and we will be at peace. This peace and security are what give us our sweet and beloved sleep.

Psalm 127:2 (NKJ) – (For so he gives his beloved sleep.)

As we drift off in fellowship with the Lord, we know that he is with us and will watch over us and sustain us as we sleep.

Psalm 3:5 (NKJ) (I lay down and slept; I awoke, for the Lord sustained me.)

I highly encourage you to start putting God first and making a place for him as you go to sleep, for this will make a huge difference in your restful, peaceful sleeping. As you sleep better, you will prosper physically, mentally, and spiritually, and sweet sleep is part of your youth being renewed like the eagles. You will sleep like a baby as they say because you are at peace, trusting and resting in the presence of your Heavenly Father.

The second reason that sweet sleep is so important is that it refreshes your physical body and allows you to heal and strengthen your body after a day's work. It is a known fact that a good night's sleep energizes and rejuvenates you physically and mentally. This is crucial for your daily activities and for serving God.

Many of you may not know that God's word mentioned sleep as much as it does. So, it was important for me to show you the scriptures, which I did, so that you know sweet sleep is one of God's promises to you as his children. By knowing this now you must thank Him and stand on this promise of sweet sleep, if you have not already done so. By knowing this promise, standing on this promise, and thanking God aloud for this promise, you have activated God's all-powerful word, and all of heaven stands behind you as God gives you his beloved sleep and your sleep becomes sweeter and sweeter!

I understand that there are a huge number of prescriptions being written for sleeping pills, and a tremendous amount of over the counter sleep aids being purchased, and these products are on the rise. There are also countless people being sent for all-night sleep studies checking for a variety of sleep disorders. I do not mean to be negative toward any of this, but I will tell you point-blank, God is the answer, not a pill or some device. God has promised that he will sustain you and give you a sweet sleep. If you are a child of God washed in the blood of Jesus, God has made provision for everything you need with sleep being one of your blessings and benefits. In this chapter, we have identified the things which attempt to rob or steal our sleep, which once again are fear, anger, anxiety, etc. We know through God's word that when we lie down meditating on him and giving a place to him that things that worry us will diminish! As we get in the habit of doing this, we know that our sleep will become sweeter and sweeter, and that our youth is being renewed. Let's look closely again at this verse.

Proverbs 3:24 (NKJ) – (When you lie down, you will not be afraid; yes, you will lie down, and your sleep will be sweet.)

As we close this chapter, I encourage you to meditate on this verse in Proverbs on which this chapter is focused. And, as you meditate and thank God, your sleep will be sweet every night. You can rest assured that He will be faithful every night making your sleep sweet.

Psalm 92:1-2 (NKJ) – (It is good to give thanks to the Lord, and to sing praises to your name O most high; To declare your loving-kindness in the morning and your faithfulness every night.)

# CHAPTER 9
## HEALTH TO THY BONES

Proverbs 17:22 (NKJ) – (A merry heart does good like a medicine, but a broken spirit dries the bones.)

As we look at the scripture above, you may be wondering if a mistake has been made in the printing of this book because the chapter on a merry heart started with the exact same verse in Proverbs. However, this is no mistake as I intended to start with this same verse. In this chapter, which is titled Health To Thy Bones, we will look at what God's word has to say about your bones and joints. It may be safe to say that most Christians don't know that your bones are discussed in the word of God. However, they are, and I think you will be greatly surprised by what our Heavenly Father tells us about our bones and joints.

God gives us very specific words on how to keep our bones healthy, and he also reveals to us what makes them unhealthy or causes them to rot or dry up. Let's look at the opening verse again, which tells us that a merry heart does good like a medicine, but a broken spirit dries the bones. As we learned in the last chapter that a merry, cheerful, joy-filled heart gives life to our bones and plays a part in our renewed youth, which is one of our benefits in Jesus.

However, we also see what the reverse does in this verse as it says that a broken spirit dries or rots the bones. Let's also look at another verse in Proverbs that speaks of rotting bones.

Proverbs 14:30 (NKJ) – (A sound heart is life to the body, but envy is rottenness to the bones.)

As we look again, it is easy to see that God is telling us and showing us that a broken spirit and envy rots or dries our bones and joints. In medical or scientific terms they will tell you that arthritis and decaying bones and joints are actually bones that are rotting or drying up. This is extremely interesting that God's word written long ago matches up with medical science. However, what is even more interesting, and also a blessing beyond words from our Heavenly Father, is that he very clearly tells us how to avoid rotting or drying bones, or as people commonly call it today arthritis. I will clearly show you through God's written word how to keep your bones healthy, but first let me share a piece of information with you. You may or may not know that scientific studies have shown many people with arthritis and joint problems have also struggled with anxiety, fear, depression, bitterness, etc. That's right, much of arthritis and aches and pains in the joints have been attributed to fear and a worried or bitter heart.

Once again, we see that science matches up with God's all-powerful word. So, it is important for us not to worry or fret.

Psalm 37:8 (NKJ) – (Cease from anger and forsake wrath; do not fret, it only causes harm.)

As we see through God's word and also medical science that fear, bitterness, envy, anger, lack of forgiveness, etc. is bad for our bones and joints and only causes harm. Now, as I promised, let's look at God's word and how to have healthy, strong bones and joints.

Proverbs 15:30 (NKJ) – (And a good report makes the bones healthy.)

This is a very powerful, to the point, verse. But, you may think, well, what is a good report? A good report is very simply, good positive words coming out of your mouth, and the best words that can come out of your mouth is God's all-powerful written word. Yes, pleasant words coming out of your mouth instead of bitter, angry, negative words strengthen your bones and make them healthy.

Proverbs 16:24 (NKJ) – (Pleasant words are like a honeycomb, sweetness to the soul, and health to the bones.)

As we say what God says about situations in our lives and others, instead of the usual negative words that people say, we are clearly giving a good report, which is health and strength to our bones. A good report out of our mouths produces faith and edifies ourselves and those around us.

If you remember back when the Israelites were in the desert, and they were grumbling and speaking negative words, they were speaking and giving a bad report, and they ended up perishing in the desert. They perished due to their bad report; however, Joshua and Caleb came out into the Promised Land because they gave a good report and trusted in God to do what he said he would do.

I will tell you a personal example of a good report that I am sure you all can relate to. Greg Williams, a good friend of mine who attends the church where I go, has a son named Sam, who is a high school football player. Sam plays fullback on the varsity team that is one of the better teams in the state of North Carolina. Sam, being a fullback, has to carry the ball quite a bit. Greg told me that Sam was having a problem in the pre-season practices with his shoulder dislocating and coming out of the joint. Greg said this was happening quite a bit, and the team orthopedic physician put Sam in a specially made brace that hopefully would protect his shoulder and keep it from dislocating.

The Orthopedic physician also said he was very concerned that this would be an ongoing problem and that Sam's shoulder would not be the same even though he was only sixteen years old.

With this being said, Greg set up a time when he and Sam could get together for prayer for Sam's healing of his shoulder. The morning before we were to meet that night at my house for prayer, God gave me a very specific word for Sam. God told me to lay hands on Sam and to speak to his bones in the name of Jesus and to his shoulders specifically. I commanded his bones to strengthen and to stay intact right now, tonight, and forever in the name of Jesus Christ of Nazareth. God told me to tell

Sam that he formed all of his parts and that he was fearfully and wonderfully made.

Psalm 139:13-14 (NKJ) – (For you formed my inward parts; you covered me in my mother's womb. I will praise you, for I am fearfully and wonderfully made; marvelous are your works, and that my soul knows very well.)

I told Sam that he needed to thank God for healing his shoulders and that he needed to give a good report with his words. I told him that he is righteous because he has accepted Jesus as his Lord and Savior of his life. I also told him to thank God that he watches over his bones, and not one of them is or will be broken.

Psalm 34:20 (NKJ) – (He guards all his bones; not one of them is broken.)

I told him to thank God, verbally out loud, throughout the day and night that he watches over his bones, not one of them is broken and never will be, in the name of Jesus. Sam left that night and received the word from me that God gave me for him. As the pre-season practice went on, Sam wore the brace the doctor gave him, and his shoulder stayed in place with no trouble. He said his shoulders felt great, and he continued to thank God that he watched over all his bones, and none of them would ever be broken.

As you can see Sam was giving a good report with his words, which is health and strength to his bones. As the actual season started, Sam felt better than ever and took the shoulder brace off and never put it back on again. He had a great football season and never had, even the slightest, trouble with his shoulders or any other part of his body the entire season, even though many of his fellow teammates picked up a variety of injuries. Sam played the following year as a fullback again, and once again had no trouble with his shoulders or any of his bones as he continued giving a good report.

Let's look once again at this scripture below, and it is now time for you to give a good report as God wants to renew your youth like the eagles and watch over your bones.

Proverbs 15:30 (NKJ) – (A good report makes the bones healthy.)

As we can clearly see, trusting and speaking God's word gives us great power and anointing, and we know that when we speak God's word with authority, all of the Kingdom of Heaven stands behind us as God watches over his word to perform it. We know that God's written word is sharper than a two-edged sword.

Since, in this chapter, we are talking about bones and joints, let's look closely at this verse, which is in the book of Hebrews.

Hebrews 4:12 (NKJ) – (For the word of God is living and powerful and sharper than any two-edged sword, piercing even to the division of soul and spirit, and of joints and marrow and is a discerner of the thoughts and intents of the heart.)

Let's look at this verse that is often quoted, using only the first part of the verse that shows how powerful the word of God actually is. We see that it is alive or living, powerful, and sharper than any two-edged sword. That is extremely penetrating or piercing, as we can see as we read on. We could spend a great deal of time on this verse, and I could probably write an entire book on this verse. However, since this chapter has to do with the health and strength of your bones, let's focus on this thought and truth. This truth and great blessing are that God's all-powerful living word actually clearly penetrates into the joints and marrow of our bodies, which is, of course, our bones as well.

There is no doubt that when we speak God's word out loud, which is a good report, it is clearly health and strength to our bones. As we see in this verse in Hebrews, it penetrates right into our bones and joints. God has shown us in these verses his wisdom and the truth of how to have strong healthy bones, which is his desire.

If we choose fear and negative words, it rots and dries our bones as scripture tells us. However, God's word out of our mouths is a good report which penetrates into our bones and promotes health and strength to our bones and joints.

To further prove this point, let's look at the third chapter in Proverbs, where God is telling us to trust him and to write his word on the tablet of our heart. After telling us to trust him and showing us the importance of knowing and standing on his word, he says this.

Proverbs 3:8 (NKJ) – (It will be health to your flesh, and strength to your bones.)

We see once again the power of God's word, and that when we know the word, speak the word, and apply it to our lives and situations, it will truly be health and strength to our bones and joints. I can't say it enough. With everything, including how to strengthen and keep our bones healthy. I truly believe as God renews our youth physically, mentally, and spiritually, healthy bones are a part of this renewing of our youth.

Let's look at one more verse where God tells us he will strengthen our bones. This verse is taken out of the book of Isaiah.

Isaiah 58:11 (NKJ) – (The Lord will guide you continually, and satisfy your soul in drought, and strengthen your bones; you shall be like a watered garden, and like a spring of water whose waters do not fail.)

These are our benefits and what God will do for us when we serve him and follow his all-powerful written word. In this list of blessings, we see again that he will strengthen our bones. As we conclude this chapter, I encourage you again to thank your Heavenly Father for he will strengthen and give health to your bones as you give a good report!

# CHAPTER 10
## EARTHING

Another huge health enhancer which is completely natural, created by God is earthing or grounding. To simplify this, we will refer to this as earthing from now on. I can't say enough good things about the practice of earthing. I first was led to this practice when I began sitting outside reading my Bible with my bare feet on the natural ground. Every morning I try to eat my breakfast outside while reading God's word. After just a couple of days of doing this in the morning with my bare feet on the ground, I noticed I had more energy and felt more relaxed. At the time I really did not know why; however, I really felt led to start spending more time outside barefoot with my feet on the natural ground or earth.

As I began to seek God on this, I was led to the scriptures, one which was in Psalm, and the other was in Proverbs. I knew God was trying to show me something about this as I was on the path of how God renews our youth. The first scripture he led me to was the 23rd chapter of Psalm verse 2.

Psalm 23:2 (NKJ) – (He makes me to lie down in green pastures.)

Even though I know this verse is clearly talking about how the Lord shepherd's us as his sheep, I knew he was also leading me to look at how he lies us down in green pastures with our bodies against the natural earth. I was also led to the book of Proverbs to chapter 19 verse 12.

Proverbs 19:12 (NKJ) – (The king's wrath is like the roaring of a lion, but his favor is like dew on the grass.)

I was getting a strong revelation of the dew on the natural grass and how it applied to my natural body, having my bare feet on the grass. I knew God was trying to show me something, and I knew that being barefoot outside on the natural ground was a natural health enhancer. Several weeks went by, and I was, for sure, in the habit of being barefoot outside. I knew that my body was not only craving it but also felt more energetic and more relaxed. One day I was surfing around on the internet, and I saw a website called earthing. As I looked on the website, it all became very clear to me why this being barefoot on the natural ground felt so good. As many of you probably know or remember from your school days that the earth has a natural electric magnetic current to it, and we, as God created human beings, also have a natural electrical system inside of us that makes our heartbeat and our bodies work. As you already know, our bodies are quite amazing.

Psalm 139:13 – 14 (NKJ) – (For you formed my inward parts; you covered me in my mother's womb. I will praise you, for I am fearfully and wonderfully made.)

Psalm 119:73 (NKJ) – (Your hands have made me and fashioned me.)

I will not get into the scientific research that I found regarding the practice of earthing, however, If you are interested you may find the book "Earthing", written by Clint Ober, Martin Zucker and Stephen Sinatra of interest to you. Especially if you want to look into the research studies on the benefits of earthing. I will tell you that the practice of earthing greatly reduces inflammation in our bodies, which is the main factor leading to most diseases. Earthing helps strengthen our immune system, strengthens our heart, regulates our hormones, increases our physical energy, and helps relax our bodies by taking away the stress. I am sure many of you can relate to how relaxing it is to feel the sand between your toes at the beach. Indeed, the beach itself is generally relaxing to people, but your feet in the sand greatly enhances this relaxed, refreshed feeling. I have now made earthing a part of each day as I spend as much time outside barefoot as possible.

I have found this fairly simple to fit into my schedule as I eat my breakfast outside and read my Bible each morning with my bare feet in the sandy soil outside my house. I also do my yard work barefoot and take walks in the woods with our dogs barefoot. Of course it is easy to sit and have your feet on the natural earth, but it does take a little getting used to, to be able to walk barefoot in the woods and work in the yard barefoot.

However, I can assure you that it is worth it. Many of you may be thinking that with your busy schedule you may not have time for the practice of earthing. So, let me offer a few suggestions. First of all, I will tell you how earthing works and where you need to do it. To earth you simply need to be barefoot on the natural ground such as grass, sand, dirt or pine straw. Concrete also is great for earthing and makes a great natural conductor as long as the concrete does not have a sealant over the surface.

Surfaces such as wood, brick, asphalt or tile will not work because it blocks the electrons from the earth and keeps them from going into your body. To practice earthing you can be sitting, standing, or walking barefoot, or as long as any part of your uncovered body comes into contact with the natural earth. For example, you could be sitting on the grass in the park with shorts on where your bare legs are coming into contact with the natural earth. Dry ground will work great for earthing; however you will notice that wet ground around water or ground during or after a rain shower greatly enhances the electrons and is a tremendous natural conductor. This is why the wet sand at the beach feels so energizing as you wade into the water or along the shoreline.

I will also suggest this as a simple way to supercharge your earthing practice. Simply wash your car on the driveway concrete in your bare feet. As you spray your vehicle with a garden hose, the water will run off onto the concrete where you are standing making the concrete wet greatly enhancing the electron conduction. You can really notice the energy going into your body if you are on the wet concrete for thirty minutes or so. You can feel the stress leaving your body.

On occasion I will wash my wife's car, my van, and my daughter's car which takes me over an hour. It amazes me how good it feels to do this in my bare feet on the wet concrete. I was never one to enjoy washing cars before, but now both my wife is happy as well as me being happy with the car washing.

For people with busy schedules washing your cars barefoot is perfect for combining earthing with your general tasks. Other ways to implement earthing is to start doing your Bible readings and devotions outside barefooted sitting in your yard. If you like to read books, do your reading outside as well as your working on your laptop or making your phone calls or even eating your breakfast, lunch or dinner outside with your bare feet on the natural earth. You can also simply relax outside and pray and talk to your Heavenly Father while outside barefoot. It may take a little adjusting your schedule at first. However, I think you will find it is well worth it once you start earthing. I try to do as much of my work outside as possible and you will also benefit from the fresh air and sunshine that God supplies us outside.

You may find it interesting that this book was written with me sitting outside barefoot, as well as my first book, the Stone and Sling. It is extremely important for me to highly emphasis that even though earthing is a natural God-given health enhancer, God is our answer to renewing our youth physically, mentally, and spiritually. We should not become obsessed with earthing or anything else. However, we should look to God as our total supply and portion for everything.

Psalm 73:26 (NKJ) – (My flesh and my heart fail, but God is my strength of my heart and my portion forever.)

Psalm 42:1 (NKJ) – (As the deer pants for the water brooks, so pants my soul for you O God.)

As you meditate on these two verses above from the book of Psalm, we must make God our portion forever and look to him for our total supply and use earthing as a natural blessing from our Heavenly Father.

I will make this interesting point. As God began to renew my youth physically, mentally, and spiritually I noticed that I seemed to enjoy being barefoot much more. I started doing the long walks in the forest while barefoot as well as doing the yard work barefoot. I truly believe that this is simply one thing God added to renew my youth. As we are called children of God, we must come to God as mere children with childlike faith.

Matthew 18:3-4 (NKJ) – (Assured, I say to you, unless you are converted and become as little children, you will by no means enter the kingdom of heaven. Therefore whoever humbles himself as this little child is the greatest in the kingdom of heaven.)

My point here is that as we humble ourselves and come to God with childlike faith, we open the door to the kingdom of God and all the things that God has for us. As God renews our youth, we are actually becoming more mature with more godly wisdom, but we also walk in more joy and peace. When this happens, we have childlike faith that overflows with the happiness of a child because we know that we are safe and secure because of our Heavenly Father.

Psalm 12:5 (NKJ) – (I will set him in the safety for which he yearns.)

As God renews our youth, we find ourselves returning to our first love, and we find ourselves returning to this state of childlike happiness and security. As God renewed my youth, like the eagles, it felt more natural and comfortable to be outside barefoot as I walked in more freedom that only our Heavenly Father can supply!

As you begin to implement the practice of earthing, you will most likely feel freer and more refreshed. At this point you probably want to ask how much time outside barefooted do you need to spend to get the positive results I am speaking of. Well, I can say that the more is probably better. But, I have read that research shows that even thirty minutes a day will greatly help you achieve better health and reduce stress. If you are only able to do thirty minutes a day earthing, I suggest you do it spending time with God by reading your Bible and praying.

One thing I will personally testify to is that earthing has helped me physically recover better after long hard workouts on my bicycle. Usually, after I take a long bicycle ride I will grab a snack and sit outside with my bare feet in the sand, which really seems to make a difference. I saw awhile back the tour De-France riders spend a lot of time earthing, which has speeded up their recovery time and also helped them sleep better. Research has also shown earthing increases physical energy and helps people sleep better.

As we close this chapter, I will mention again that I highly suggest that you try earthing. However, its blessing is something natural God has given us. But, we must put God first and always look to him because he is the one who renews our youth like the eagles as this is one of our benefits as his children!

# CHAPTER 11
## BLESSED FEET

1 Samuel 2:9 (NKJ) – (He will guard the feet of his saints.)

In this chapter, we will discuss the importance of the feet and the paths they take both spiritually and physically. This is an extremely important chapter, and the feet play a huge role when it comes to renewing your youth God's way! The word of God has a lot to say about our feet and the importance of them.

Look closely at the verse above in 1 Samuel, where God tells us he guards the feet of his saints. Who are his saints? His saints are you and I if we have made Jesus Lord and Savior of our lives. Just think, one of our promises from the Lord is that he guards our feet. This is a truly powerful blessing!

You may say, how does he do this? That's a great question so, let's look at how he does this both spiritually and physically as I have truly learned firsthand. Please look closely at the verse below, as I believe the Lord will reveal some powerful truths that you have probably never thought of.

Proverbs 4:26 (NKJ) – (Ponder the path of your feet and let all your ways be established.)

First of all, we can see that we must watch where we go and don't let our feet carry us into temptation and harmful situations that will cause us harm.

Proverbs1:16 (NKJ) – (My son, do not walk in the way with them, keep your foot from their path; For their feet run to evil, and they make haste to shed blood.)

We must truly ponder our paths and keep our feet grounded in Jesus, which will keep us from slipping.

Psalm 73:2 (NKJ) – (But as for me, my feet had almost slipped; I had nearly lost my foothold.)

If we look back at the second part of the verse in Proverbs chapter 4 verse 26, we can see if we do watch and ponder the paths of our feet that (All your ways will be established.) This is a wonderful blessing as all of our ways will be established! Brothers and sisters, we must watch our paths and thank God aloud that he guards our feet. We can also see, in his word, that our feet are blessed as we do his kingdom work and share the good news of Jesus with those around us.

Isaiah 52:7 (NKJ) – (How beautiful on the mountains are the feet of those who bring good news, who proclaim peace, who bring good tidings, who proclaim salvation, who say to Zion, your God reigns.)

The Lord truly blesses our feet and gives us the ability to climb to new heights, through him, as we put him first. We can accomplish our personal destiny the Lord has called us into as he gives us the ability to go places we never thought we could or would go without him. No matter how high or rugged the route looks, he enables us to climb to the top on hinds feet just like the deer.

Psalm 18:33 (KJV) – (He maketh my feet like hinds feet and setteth me upon my high places.)

Habakkuk 3:19 (KJV) – (The Lord God is my strength, and he will make my feet like hinds feet, and he will make me to walk upon mine high places.)

If you ever look at the hinds feet of a deer, you can see why their footing is so good on rough mountain terrain and how they can dart in any direction so quickly and surefooted. This is what the Lord does for us when we trust in him wholeheartedly and ponder the path of our feet and keep them from evil. The

Lord makes us surefooted, but places the ungodly on slippery ground.

Psalm 35:6 (NKJ) – (Let their way be dark and slippery, and let the angel of the Lord pursue them.)

Psalm 73:18 (NIV)– (Surely you place them on slippery ground; You cast them down to ruin.)

We have discussed how the Lord will guard our feet and protect us spiritually from going down the wrong path when we look to him and follow his instructions. Now, I would like to open your eyes to a very important part of renewing and retaining your youth and longevity in the physical realm!

First of all, your feet are extremely important and complex. There are twenty-six bones and thirty-three joints in your feet. You also have quite a control panel of nerves at the bottom of your feet, which send messages to your muscles, which help control and adjust your balance and gait. Your feet are truly fearfully and wonderfully made.

Psalm 139:14 (NKJ) – (I will praise you, for I am fearfully and wonderfully made.)

With this being said, I have come to truly understand that our feet play a huge role in our health and wellbeing! In fact, I feel strongly that the Lord has shown me a huge deception, under the sun, that is literally taking away many people's mobility and physical health before their time. This deception is a snare to trap your feet and keep them from functioning the way God designed them to function.

Let's think about a natural snare in the woods. A snare is designed to catch your foot, and a well-placed snare is covered where it can't be seen well. The devil wishes and tries to snare us in many ways, spiritually, mentally, and physically. The devil, our adversary, is also called the fowler in some verses where he is trying to snare our feet.

Psalm 91:3 (NKJ) – (Surely he shall deliver you from the fowlers snare.)

Psalm 124:7 (NKJ) – (Our soul has escaped as a bird from the snare of the fowlers; the snare is broken, and we have escaped.)

You might be saying at this point, well, this is interesting but, what does this have to do with my feet, and how am I being deceived? Well, let's first look back at how God created us. God created us barefoot, where our feet could totally feel the ground.

Back then, the feet were also the main mode of transportation. In some countries and regions today, there are still people who don't wear and have never worn shoes. Research has shown that these people also have the healthiest feet, plus they report very little, if any, joint issues.

God created us barefoot where the feet could be feet. When they weren't barefoot, they wore a FLAT sandal that still kept them in a barefoot way of walking and standing, where the foot could function as a natural foot. They did not walk and move in a rigid thick padded shoe with arch supports. Nor did they have a lifted heel and a narrow toe box jamming their toes together!

All of these things I just mentioned keep the foot from functioning properly, plus they weaken the feet and are a total deviation to the way God designed our feet to function and work. Therefore, this has become a snare that can trap your feet and keep you from being all God created you to be, by hurting your future and long-term mobility.

However, God wants to deliver you from that snare and put you on the right path to renewing and retaining your youth. God is literally giving you this wisdom and blessing you in a powerful way!

Proverbs 4:10–12 (NKJ) – (Hear my son and receive my sayings, and the years of your life will be many. I have taught you in the way of wisdom; I have led you in right paths. When you walk, your steps will not be hindered, and when you run, you will not stumble.)

Let's look briefly at some of the drawbacks and problems with most of the modern-day shoes.

No. 1- They have a lifted and elevated heel, which tilts you forward, and throws your whole body out of alignment, placing pressure on your back. Just think for a moment and picture the elevated heels on most shoes that place you in a slightly downhill forward tilted position. You would not want to build your house unlevel with a tilt, so why then would you want to wear shoes that tilt you into an unlevel position.

No. 2- Most shoes have a tight, narrow toe box, which keeps your toes from spreading out and balancing us correctly. The narrow toe box not only keeps us from our best alignment and balance but, over time, can make our toes crooked, jammed together, and nonfunctional, which can impact our entire skeletal system.

Just think that when your toes are properly splayed and aligned, you have better balance because your base is wider and better rooted! Just like Jesus wants you to be well-rooted and grounded in love, I believe he also wants your feet and toes to be well-rooted and grounded the way He created your feet to be.

Ephesians 3:17 (NKJ) – (That Christ may dwell in your hearts through faith; That you, being rooted and grounded in love.)

Colossians 2:7 (NKJ) – (Rooted and built up in him and established in the faith, as you have been taught, abounding in it with Thanksgiving.)

No. 3- Most shoes have built-in arch supports that raise your arches, trying to keep them from dropping or falling. The practice of using arch supports is extremely widespread as arch supports are sold everywhere. Arch supports are either already built in your shoes or sold in stores or even customized by well-meaning health care providers.

Please understand that a large percentage of people do have weak fallen arches. However, much of this is because their feet and arches have weakened, over time, due to bad shoes and their arches not having to engage themselves.

With flat shoes, flat sandals or barefoot, the arches are forced to activate and engage the way God intended them to engage! The arches are more than willing and able to engage, and YES, they can be built back up again! Praise the Lord! Please understand that arch supports are exactly what they are called, they are arch SUPPORTS which basically make your arches lazy by knowing they have the support and don't have to work the way God created them to work.

They can overtime become strong again and bear their own load.

Galatians 6:5 (NKJ) – (For each one shall bear his own load.)

It is my prayer and hope that what I said about your physical feet makes sense and motivates you to take better care of your feet the way God intended. If it does, you are probably thinking, what should I do, and how should I go about it safely? These are great questions, and I would be concerned if you didn't ask them.

In the last part of this chapter, I will reveal to you how to safely get started with the process of regaining your foot health. Even though this could easily be an entire book in itself, I will simply show you how to get going and a safe path to travel on. Please remember, as a child of God, that God is with you. His will is for your feet to function the way he created them to function! And your benefit is renewed youth, including healthier, stronger feet.

Remember when the Israelites were in the wilderness and walking much of the time in thin flat sandals with no arch supports and no heel lifts? They were able to walk the way God made their feet to function. As you probably remember, they were in the wilderness for forty years with no foot issues. How do I know this, and why didn't they have foot issues? Because God sustained them, and He is the same God who will sustain YOU as you look to him!

Nehemiah 9:21 (KJV) – (For forty years you sustained them in the wilderness; they lacked nothing; their clothes did not wear out nor did their feet become swollen.)

We now have a better covenant with God since Jesus died on the cross for us. To start your journey on the right path to developing strong, healthy, more functional feet, we will first have to ease you into barefoot walking. If you are already a barefoot person, that is great, and I encourage you to do more barefoot living.

If you are new to going barefoot, simply start by walking barefoot around your house or yard some. Remember, if you have worn shoes with arch supports and a lifted heel for years and years, the barefoot walking will feel quite different. This is because now your foot muscles are engaging, and your body is in a whole different alignment. Simply stay barefoot awhile each day walking around your house or yard doing a little bit of work like you would normally do.

Be careful not to push things at first because the wearing of wrong shoes for so long is like basically putting your feet in casts, which have caused your feet to be deconditioned. Continue going barefoot for longer periods and also get into the practice of wiggling and manipulating your toes as much as possible. If you can't wiggle all your toes at first, don't worry; keep trying as this motor skill will come back.

Also, be aware that your feet might get a little sore, or even your legs and back. Don't worry; this can be very normal at first. If something causes you pain, of course back off. However, some slight discomfort is very normal as your feet and ankles begin to strengthen and become more mobile. Also, remember that it takes time to truly rehab and strengthen all the muscles, ligaments, and tendons of the feet and lower legs.

I will give you an example of the protocol that I personally used to break into a barefoot lifestyle. For the last five years or so, I have been doing some barefoot walking and working in the yard. Most days, I was taking a 2-mile barefoot walk in the woods on a dirt path, which felt great. However, I was still working in boots during the day five days a week, which had arch support, plus the back heels were slightly elevated as most boots and shoes are.

About a year and a half ago, I went to either barefoot or wearing a completely flat boot or sandal with light padding in the footbed. Even though it took me some time to safely adapt to this type of natural barefoot lifestyle, I would never go back again to wearing traditional shoes.

I now do a lot of tough hiking and trail running in a light, thin, flexible sandal similar to the ones they wore in Biblical times. Before I started any hiking or running in my barefoot sandals I did this preparation. I walked slowly over 100 miles barefoot on a dirt path. After that I walked more briskly for over 100 miles on the path. With well over 200 miles walking completely barefoot, I started jogging lightly with my sandals on for about 400 yards or so a day. After that, I slowly, but surely, increased my distance and speed.

I am not at all suggesting that you start running or hiking barefoot, I simply wanted to show you how I safely trained my feet for a natural barefoot lifestyle which God has blessed me with! I also want in particular to briefly touch on two parts of the lower legs which going barefoot will greatly enhance. However, you will also want to, once again, start slowly to keep from straining or overworking these areas.

The first is the Achilles tendon, which runs from your calf muscles to your heel bone. The Achilles tendon will get slightly stretched and lengthened from going barefoot, which is great. However, you must not try to do this all at once. You must let it lengthen and strengthen, little-by-little as you progress with your barefoot renewing.

The second is the great toe or big toe. The big toe, as we will call it, is extremely important to our walking gait and balance. Barefoot walking and working barefoot will work the big toe and strengthen and mobilize it. However, like the Achilles tendon you must take it slow and not overwork or strain it. With a little bit of barefoot lifestyle, your big toes will improve your balance and walking gait.

Barefoot training will put you on the natural path God not only planned for you, but originally placed you on.

Psalm 119:105 (NKJ) – (Your word is a lamp for my feet, a light on my path.)

So start kicking off your shoes, and let God start renewing your youth by placing your feet on level ground!

Psalm 26:12 (NIV) – (My feet stand on level ground; In the great congregation, I will praise the Lord.)

I want to add a couple of websites and products that I highly recommend that can greatly help you get on the right path to true foot health and the renewing of your feet to how God created them to be!

Also, I want you to know that I get nothing from these companies for mentioning them other than knowing that their products will help you renew and retain your foot health.

1- Lems Shoes – Lems makes a variety of minimal footwear that allows your feet to move like God intended them to move. All their footwear is extremely flexible, comfortable and has an extremely wide toe box to allow your toes room to splay and function properly. They even have a minimal boot called a Boulder Boot, which I personally wear several days a week when I can't go barefoot or in a sandal. The Boulder boot is great for anyone who works outside and has to have foot protection while still having a minimal natural feel to their feet.

2- Minimal Sandals – As you probably know, I prefer sandals if I have to wear anything on my feet. Remember, sandals are what everyone wore in Biblical times, including Jesus. There are many verses in God's word, where sandals are mentioned. Including the one below where God himself tosses his sandal!

Psalm 60:8 (NKJ) – (Moab is my washbasin; on Edom, I toss my sandal; Over Philistia I shout in triumph.)

I think it is safe to assume that the apostles, Jesus, and God himself, still wear sandals. Why?

Hebrews 13:8 (NKJ) – (Jesus Christ is the same yesterday, and today, and forever.)

Here are three companies that make minimal sandals that you can run, hike, or simply wear for everyday use. I have and still do wear sandals from all three of these companies.

1- Shamma Sandals – Shamma Sandals.com

2- Bedrock Sandals – Bedrock Sandals.com

3- Luna Sandals – Luna Sandals.com

Note- If you want a sandal with a little more padding, Luna sandals make a couple of their sandals with a bit more thickness and padding in the footbed.

One additional product I will mention is Correct Toes™, which is a great innovative product that will help space and properly realign your toes to the way God intended them to be spaced and aligned. Many people now, because of wearing bad shoes, have crooked toes, jammed together, and improperly splayed. Correct Toes™ is to your toes like braces are to your teeth. However, Correct Toes™ are comfortable and can be worn or taken off anytime you wish. Correct Toes.com.

Proverbs 3:6 (NIV) – (In all your ways submit to him, and he will make your paths straight.)

# CHAPTER 12
## GIRD THY LOINS

Nahum 2:1 (KJV) – (He that dasheth in pieces is come up before your face. Man the fort! Watch the road! Make thy loins strong, fortify thy power mightily.)

In this chapter, we will look at the Biblical importance of your loins, both physically and mentally. In fact, the renewing of your loins is important to God and is part of how God renews your youth like the eagles, which is one of your benefits you must claim and thank Him for!

Let's look first at your loins in the physical sense. As we look at the verse above in Nahum, we see the Lord saying to prepare ourselves as an attacker is coming. He tells us to make our loins strong, which will actually fortify and summon our strength and power! You may be asking what or where are our loins first of all, and how do I gird or strengthen them? Well, first of all, let me tell you a very interesting fact. The Psoas muscle is the only muscle in the entire body that connects the upper and lower body together. Also, guess what the word Psoas means in Greek? It means loins, and much of the Bible is written in Greek, which is a very interesting fact in itself.

So, our loins are the very center or core of our bodies which God tells us to strengthen, to fortify, to gird. In the physical realm, it is highly important to strengthen and keep this area healthy because, for one, it keeps our back and spine protected from injury and aging too quickly. So, therefore, we need to strengthen, fortify, and gird our loins to keep our back and spine healthy and youthful.

By doing this, we can renew our backs and spine and actually make them more youthful! Even though I could probably write an entire book on strengthening and girding our loins, we will focus on the back in this chapter. Probably about everyone out there has at one time, or another pulled a back muscle or had a back issue that has slowed them down.

I want you to know that God cares about you, your back, and all of you, for he has made you and formed you for good works!

Ephesians 2:10 (NKJ) – (For we are his workmanship, created in Christ Jesus for good works, which God prepared beforehand that we should walk in them.)

Psalm 139:13 (NKJ) – (For you formed my inward parts, you covered me in my mother's womb.)

It's time to gird your loins and start taking care of your back for your youthful longevity because your entire body is the temple of the Holy Spirit who wants to use your healthy, or soon to be healthy body, for good works!

1 Corinthians 6:19-20 (NIV) – (Do you not know that your bodies are temples of the Holy Spirit, who is in you, whom you have received from God? You are not your own; you were bought at a price. Therefore honor God with your bodies.)

As I mentioned before, this is not an exercise book, but, in this chapter, I will speak briefly on decompression of the spine, which research has shown helps keep your back healthy by keeping your discs from compressing together. Spinal decompression not only helps keep your discs from touching but, it also helps hydrate the discs and lengthens tight muscles and fascia keeping them supple.

In short, spinal decompression helps keep your back more youthful, the way God intended your back to be.

Job 33:25 (NIV) – (Let their flesh be renewed like a child's; Let them be restored as in the days of their youth.)

Let's look at a few ways in which you can decompress your back and make it more supple and youthful.

1– Inversion tables are quite popular and have been used for many, many years now. I used a Teeter™ inversion table from time to time, and they are quite user-friendly and safe. Also, with a Teeter™ inversion table, you can invert at different angles, which allows you to ease into total inversion, slowly, if you are uncomfortable at first.

Generally speaking, they suggest about 3 minutes daily of total inversion, which will greatly help decompress your spine and make it more supple and relaxed! You can also break up the 3 minutes of inversion into different time frames until you get used to the feeling of being upside down.

I don't get anything for mentioning the Teeter™ brand inversion table, by the way, except for knowing that it can help keep and make your back more supple and youthful. Their website is Teeter.com

2– Next, I will briefly mention the Yoga Trapeze™, which I personally own. If you are not a Yoga person, don't let the name Yoga concern you. The Yoga Trapeze™ is user-friendly, and you don't have to be a yoga person to comfortably and safely use the trapeze. You also don't have to be a circus performer as the word trapeze might make you think.

The Yoga Trapeze™ not only allows you to invert but also to have a complete range of motion with your hips and legs. This not only enables you to decompress your spine but to also get great mobility in your hips and legs as well. It also has handles where you can use your shoulders and arms. The Yoga Trapeze™ will really help you strengthen and stretch your loins and renew your youth in this area. Their website is Yogabody.com

3– The last way of decompressing your spine that I will mention is simply hanging from a pull-up bar. This, of course, is quite simple. However, you do need to have a bit of grip strength. Hanging from a pull-up bar will decompress your spine and lengthen your back muscles.

I will show you how to enhance the benefits of this drill greatly. As you grip the bar with your arms extended at about shoulder-width, be sure to let your feet dangle and touch the floor slightly. Letting your feet dangle and slightly touch the ground will cause your pelvis to drop and stretch more.

As you grasp the bar with your arms extended and feet dangling, hold your breath and create as much tension in your body as possible for about 5 seconds. Now while still hanging onto the bar with your grip strength, relax and let the tension go in the rest of your body as you release your breath and breath normally again. You will feel a lengthening and stretching of your entire back and hip region from doing this. This will decompress your spine by creating a safe, natural form of traction. Try to hold onto the bar for about 30 seconds or so.

Feel free to repeat this exercise several times a day if you can! I believe you will also find that by decompressing daily, you will help muscle imbalances in your loins or core region. Often times, for example, one set of muscles on one side will become stronger or tighter than the other side, which will pull your pelvis out of alignment.

This kind of muscle imbalance can cause discomfort in your back, hips, glutes, or even in your groin area. These muscle imbalances can pull against one another, causing a lot of tension and possibly cause an uneven awkward gait as your muscles and alignment are not moving smoothly and are not equally yoked!

Amos 3:3 (NKJ) – (Can two walk together unless they have agreed?)

Deuteronomy 22:10 (NKJ) – (You shall not plow with an ox and a donkey together.)

As we look at the last verse saying not to plow with a donkey and ox yoked together, we can see also how this could apply to our own walking gait. For example, with the ox and donkey, the donkey steps and moves faster, but the ox moves slower but is much stronger. The ox also can pull longer with better endurance.

As you can picture these two yoked together and moving forward, pulling a plow, you can imagine how choppy and awkward they would move due to the imbalance. This can also be true with our movement and gait patterns. However, decompression can drastically help muscle imbalances. Why? Because decompression overtime will lengthen and relax the tighter compressed area more than the supple areas. For example, let's say your right-side muscles are tighter than the left side muscles and pulling your balance off. The decompression will stretch the right-side muscles more than the left because they need to be stretched and lengthened more to bring you back into balance and make you more evenly yoked in your loin area.

I hope I have encouraged you to take care of your backs as well as encouraged you to try decompression to help restore and retain a strong, healthy youthful back.

Now let's look at the importance of girding the loins of our minds!

1 Peter 1:13 (NKJ) – (Therefore gird up the loins of your mind, be sober and rest your hope fully upon the grace that is to be brought to you at the revelation of Jesus Christ.)

We can see by the verse above that we must keep our minds on Jesus, put him first, and stay zealous for the things of God. If we gird the loins of our minds by keeping our focus on Jesus, we will accomplish our destiny and be all God created us to be! I highly encourage you to keep your focus and be zealous for the things of God and be bold and arise to your calling. Gird up your loins because God goes before you and is with you!

Jeremiah 1:17 (KJV) – (Thou therefore gird up thy loins and arise and speak unto them all that I command thee; Be not dismayed at their faces, lest I confound thee before them.)

As we close this chapter on girding our loins, I want you to meditate on the below verse in Acts, where Peter was let out of prison by the angel. Notice the angel told Peter to gird thyself, which means be ready and prepare yourself and to bind his sandals, which means he would be moving and going on a journey!

I believe God is breaking you out of your prison, which are the things holding you back. He is also telling you to gird and prepare yourself and put your sandals on because he is ready to take you on a journey and take you to places you have never been before. I believe God is taking you into a new land, A land that flows with milk and honey, and he is calling you into your destiny where you will be all that he created you to be! Amen and Amen!

Acts 12:8 (KJV) – (And the angel said unto him, gird thyself and bind thy sandals. And so he did. And he saith unto him, cast thy garment about thee and follow me.)

# CHAPTER 13
## LONG LIFE AND LENGTH OF DAYS

Proverbs 3:2 (NKJ) – (For length of days and long life and peace they will add to you.)

Proverbs 3:16 (NKJ) – (Length of days is in her right hand, in her left hand are riches and honor.)

In this chapter, I will show you, biblically, how to achieve a long life and length of days as the verses above tell us. This is a large part of having your youth renewed God's way, which once again is one of your benefits as a child of God washed in the blood of Jesus. Long life is, of course, a huge blessing that everyone hopes for and seeks.

In this chapter, I will show you the path to long life and length of days based on the all-powerful word of God! On top of having a long life, you can also have your strength equal your days with your days being many!

Deuteronomy 33:25 (NIV) – (The bolts of your gates will be iron and bronze, and your strength will equal your days.)

Does God have an anti-aging plan or what some might call a fountain of youth? I believe without a doubt, yes, he does, and it is all through his written word. I will also tell you that this plan must be done God's way, just as the book title reads, Renew Your Youth God's Way. Even though man, through research and trial and error, comes up with different things that can enhance one's health and well-being, man truly doesn't know or understand how to renew one's youth and vitality very long. For as it is written:

1 Corinthians 3:19 (NKJ) – (For the wisdom of this world is foolishness with God. For it is written, He taketh the wise in their own craftiness.)

Proverbs 26:12 (NKJ) (Do you see a person wise in their own eyes? There is more hope for a fool than for them.)

I am not saying that we can't learn health and longevity principles from man, and at times some of these principles line up with what God is saying in his written word. However often, it does not, and it is God who decides and God alone who decides the number of our years and days and God who also can extend them!

Psalm 139:16 (NKJ) – (Your eyes saw my substance being yet unformed. And in Your book they all were written, the days fashioned for me, when as yet there were none of them.)

I will never forget one morning when I was spending time with the Lord, and he said to me, John, do you know what my answer to 911 is? Of course, 911 is the dialing number for emergencies such as medical, fire, and rescue and police emergencies. Most people think of 911, and these emergencies strike fear into them. However, it is not these situations that decide our destiny and our life span but, God alone. Please look closely at the verse below and let it saturate into your spirit!

Proverbs 9:11 (NKJ) – (For by me your days will be multiplied and years of life will be added to you.)

As you look at this powerful verse, did you notice what the number is? It is 911; this is no accident or coincidence. It is God showing you that it is not man, situations or emergencies, that decides your days and years lived, but it is almighty God, the one who created you, heaven and earth who decides! Also, you can clearly see in God's unsearchable wisdom he wrote this verse through King Solomon long ago, knowing that in today's modern times, the number 911 would be for emergency calls.

Isn't this powerful and great news that God says FOR BY ME your days will be multiplied, and years of life will be added to you. Notice that God not only can give you a long life, but he also can and will extend your days and years! Now would be a great time to praise and thank the Lord for this powerful blessing. At this point, you may be wondering what is required, and what does it take for you to activate this powerful benefit? This is a very good question to ask so, let's look at how we can and WILL do this.

First of all, we must remember and understand it is God's way and God who does this, so we must seek him and listen to him to achieve a long life and length of days.

Proverbs 1:5 (NKJ) – (A wise man will hear and increase learning, and a man of understanding will attain wise counsel.)

Proverbs 4:10 (NKJ) – (Hear my son and receive my sayings and the years of your life will be many.)

As we look at these verses, we can see that once again, we must solely look to God, trust in him and his word, and as we begin doing this, we will not only activate this benefit but also understand this benefit. We will move forward into our personal destiny and become all that God created us to be.

Jesus loves you dearly and desires that you fulfill your destiny and live a long healthy, happy life here on earth. When Jesus went to the cross and died for you, YOU received many benefits once you receive him as Lord and Savior. Of course, the forgiveness of sins is crucial but, there are many others as well. Jesus died to give us life more abundantly. Two of these benefits are divine health and long life, which are part of your salvation as believers.

Psalm 91:16 (NKJ) – (With long life I will satisfy him and show him my salvation.)

I truly believe as we look with our spiritual eyes, we can see a great revelation in this. Jesus died at 33 years old in the prime of his life, so we don't have to. Jesus could have died on the cross at age 90 or 190 but, he died a premature death, so we don't have to. I believe he bore this for us also, so we must see this and thank him. Praise the Lord!

Psalm 150:2 (NKJ) – (Praise him for his mighty acts; praise him according to his excellent greatness.)

As we seek God, put him first, and let his word saturate our mind, body, and spirit, I have found that we will walk in all these benefits and experience a long healthy life.

1 Kings 3:14 (NKJ) – (So if you walk in my ways, to keep my statutes and my commandments, as your father David walked, then I will lengthen your days.)

Deuteronomy 11:9 (NAS) – (So that you may prolong your days on the land which the Lord swore to your fathers to give them and to their descendants, a land flowing with milk and honey.)

Proverbs 10:27 (NKJ) – (The fear of the Lord prolongs days, but the years of the wicked will be shortened.)

As we are focusing on how to live a long, healthy life and how to prolong our days as scripture shows us, let's also look at what can shorten our life span and our days. It is evident that by doing the opposite of what God says, we are very prone and likely to cut our years and days short. First, let's look back at the last verse, where the fear of the Lord prolongs life. Look now at the last part of the verse where it says (but the years of the wicked will be shortened.)

We can see that being wicked will shorten our lives. Look below at two more examples of this.

Psalm 55:23 (NKJ) – (But you O God, shall bring them down to the pit of destruction; Bloodthirsty and deceitful men shall not live out half their days; But, I will trust in you.)

Ecclesiastes 7:17 (NIV) – (Be not overly wicked, neither be a fool. Why should you die before your time)?

I also felt strongly led to touch on the importance of respecting and honoring parents. Of course, this is one of the ten commandments. As there are many verses that discuss the blessings that go with honoring parents, there are also some verses telling about the perils of not honoring parents. Let's look first at the blessings and how they produce a long life!

Exodus 20:12 (NKJ) – (Honor your father and your mother, that your days may be prolonged in the land which the Lord your God gives you.)

Colossians 3:20 (NKJ) – (Children, be obedient to your parents in all things, for this is well-pleasing to the Lord.)

Ephesians 6:1-3 (NKJ) – (Children obey your parents in the Lord, for this is right. Honor your father and mother which is the first commandment with a promise; That it may be well with you and you may live long on the earth.)

What is this promise again for honoring your father and mother? It may go well with you, and you will have a long life! Now let's look at some verses regarding treating parents poorly.

Proverbs 30:17 (NKJ) – (The eye that mocketh his father and despiseth to obey his mother, the ravens of the valley shall pick it out and the young eagles shall eat it.)

Proverbs 20:20 (NKJ) – (Whoever curses his father or his mother, his lamp shall be put out in deep darkness.)

As we focus on the two verses above, they can be very sobering and thought-provoking, to say the least. However, the Lord impressed upon me to add these verses to this chapter on a long life and length of days. The above verses can appear to be very bad news for many of us. Many of us have not treated our parents well and disrespected them, and these verses can apply to us. However, I highly encourage you, if this applies to you, to repent right now and ask your parents for forgiveness and start over and start cultivating a better relationship with them this very day. You may be saying my parents have abused me, and I can't be around them. If so, pray for them and ask God what to do as far as your future relationship with them, for this is God's will!

Matthew 7:7 (NKJ) – (Ask, and it shall be given you; Seek, and ye shall find; Knock, and it shall be opened to you.)

You also may have treated your parents badly, and they are dead now, and you can't go back and change your relationship with them. If this is so, I still have good news for you as God is just to forgive you of this the same way; he will forgive you for any of your sins. If you confess them and ask for forgiveness in Jesus' name, YOU will be forgiven!

1 John 1:9 (NKJ) – (If we confess our sins, he is faithful and just to forgive us our sins and to cleanse us from all unrighteousness.)

Psalm 32:5 (NIV) – (Then I acknowledged my sin to you and did not hide my iniquity. I said, I will confess my transgressions to the Lord, and you forgave the guilt of my sin.)

Psalm 103:3 (NKJ) – (Who forgives all your iniquities, who heals all your diseases.)

I highly encourage you right now to ask forgiveness in Jesus' name. If you have dishonored your parents, no matter if they are dead or living. Asking for forgiveness for any sin, and then moving forward without feeling any condemnation, is a huge part of having your youth renewed and experiencing a long healthy, happy life!

Romans 8:1 (NKJ) – (There is therefore now no condemnation to them which are in Christ Jesus, who walk not after the flesh, but after the spirit.)

Let's look at a few examples of people who had their youth renewed as well as years added to their lives, and also their strength equaled their days. We will also look at why this happened to them and how you, too, can achieve this blessing in your life!

Let's look first at Caleb, who was with Moses and Joshua in the desert, trying to enter the Promised Land. Caleb was 40 years old when they started their journey to the Promised Land and 85 years old when he was given the mountain he was promised.

Caleb was as strong at 85 as he was at 40, plus he still had his motivation and his heart followed God wholeheartedly! This is what Caleb had to say.

Joshua 14:10-12 (NKJ) – (Now then, just as the Lord promised, he has kept me alive for forty-five years since the time he said this to Moses, while Israel moved about in the wilderness. So here I am today, eighty-five years old! I am still as strong today as the day Moses sent me out; I am just as vigorous to go out to battle now as I was then. Now give me this mountain the Lord promised me that day.)

We can see without a doubt that Caleb's strength truly equaled his days, as he at 85 years old had the same strength he had at age 40! He even said he was just as vigorous now at age 85 even to go out to battle. We see he asked for the mountain and land that was originally promised to him. His strength equaled his days physically, mentally, and spiritually. We also know that Caleb was surrounded by grumblers who were constantly complaining about their conditions in the desert.

Just imagine that you were in the desert for all those years, like Caleb was, complaining the entire time. Also, remember it was the desert, which was hot and extremely uncomfortable. However, Caleb kept his faith and all aspects of his strength the entire time, and still entered into the land God had promised, a land flowing with milk and honey.

How did Caleb maintain his faith and strength all those years in that incredibly harsh environment? This is a great question which God himself answers in the below verse.

Numbers 14:24 (NIV) – (But because my servant Caleb has a different spirit and follows me wholeheartedly, I will bring him into the land he went to, and his descendants will inherit it.)

Caleb had a different spirit, kept his faith, and did not grumble even though he was surrounded by grumblers. How did he do this? He followed God wholeheartedly and trusted in God's promise. We know how crucial it is to keep our hearts right, which will keep us trusting in God! God is truly the strength of our hearts.

Proverbs 4:23 (NIV) – (Above all else, guard your heart, for everything you do flows from it.)

Psalm 73:26 (NKJ) – (My flesh and my heart may fail, but God is the strength of my heart and my portion forever.)

We can learn a lot from the story of Caleb entering into the Promised Land, even in such a harsh environment physically because of the desert heat and conditions and also mentally because of all the grumbling around him. This story of Caleb is great news for you and me because it clearly shows you that YOU will achieve your Promised Land and personal destiny no matter what your circumstances are, if only you will keep your eyes on God's promises and keep your heart on the things of God!

I will say it again. YOU WILL achieve all God has for you regardless of the conditions and obstacles around you if you follow God wholeheartedly and trust in his word!

Psalm 119:11 (NIV) – (I have hidden your word in my heart that I might not sin against you.)

We will look at an example now where God multiplied days and added years to the life of King Hezekiah. The prophet Isaiah tells King Hezekiah to get his house in order because he is going to die.

Isaiah 38:1 (NIV) – (In those days, Hezekiah became ill and was at the point of death. The prophet Isaiah, son of Amos, went to him and said, "This is what the Lord says; put your house in order because you are going to die; you will not recover.")

After hearing this news, Hezekiah wept and cried out to the Lord, reminding him how he has kept a loyal heart and done right in his sight. Just like Caleb, who ASKED for the mountain, and God gave him the mountain. Hezekiah asked to live, and God granted his request and lengthened his days!

Isaiah 38:5 (NIV) – (Go tell Hezekiah, "This is what the Lord, the God of your father David says; I have heard your prayer and seen your tears; I will add fifteen years to your life.")

God heard and granted both Caleb's and Hezekiah's requests, the same way he wants to answer and heed your requests. Remember, both Caleb and Hezekiah were mightily used by God. Why? Scripture tells us they both had loyal hearts to God and trusted in him and his promises! They were not only used by God but, they experienced a long life and length of days.

Let's look at another situation where God renewed someone's youth in a mighty way. Sarah, the wife of Abraham, was 90 years old when Isaac was born. Long before Sarah conceived Isaac, God made her and Abraham this promise.

Genesis 17:16 (NIV) – (I will bless her and will surely give you a son by her. I will bless her so that she will be the mother of nations; Kings of peoples will come to her.)

Yes, Sarah was used in a mighty way by God, and her youth was renewed even at age 90 as she bore a son. Why did this happen, and why was God able to use Sarah for his kingdom in such a powerful way? She had faith in God and stood on his promise to her!

Hebrews 11:11 (NIV) – (And by faith even Sarah, who was past childbearing age, was enabled to bear children because she considered him faithful who had made the promise.)

Once again, we see an example of someone having faith and standing on God's promise with a loyal heart. Let's look at one more example of long life and their strength equaling their days.

Deuteronomy 34:7 (NKJ) – (Moses was one hundred and twenty years old when he died. His eyes were not dim nor his natural vigor diminished.)

This verse is so simple, yet so, so powerful. Moses died at the age of 120 in perfect health! God blessed Moses with long-life, length of days, as well as his strength equaling his days. You might ask, what did Moses die of? He died in perfect health and died because he had fulfilled his assignment, destiny, and his days.

As we look at these four examples in God's word, we see they all trusted God's word, we see they trusted God, had loyal hearts and also claimed the promises they were given by asking God for them!

My brothers and sisters, you may have everything God has created for you by asking him and standing on his word and promises. Also, as we look at these four examples, we can see they were before Jesus died on the cross for you and me. We can now have life and life more abundantly. Yes we have a far better covenant than Moses, Caleb, Sarah, and Hezekiah! As you move forward with God wholeheartedly and saturate yourself in God's word and ways, you will be satisfied with long life, length of days, and your strength will equal your days as the Lord will show you his Salvation!

Also, remember it is not man, nor circumstances, nor obstacles that decide your destiny and years lived but, it is God alone as it is written!

Proverbs 9:11 (NKJ) – (For by me your days will be multiplied, and years of life will be added to you.) AMEN AND AMEN!

# CHAPTER 14
## WHAT RENEWING YOUR YOUTH IS NOT

1 Corinthians 6:18 (NKJ) – (Flee sexual immorality. Every sin that a man does is outside the body, but he who commits sexual immorality sins against his own body.)

Even though this chapter is very short, and I will not go into great detail on the subject, I felt that it is crucial to touch on this. I also felt led by the Lord to add this chapter to clear up any possible confusion one may have when they hear the phrase renewing your youth. My point here is this, someone who is thinking on the subject of renewing your youth might confuse this with going through a second childhood or a midlife crisis.

Often, when someone thinks of a second childhood or a midlife crisis, they may picture someone who starts acting childish and possibly immoral. Men and women, trying to live a second childhood, often begin to look at the opposite sex forsaking their spouse and even committing adultery or other immoral acts. Renewing your youth, God's way, is the farthest thing from living a second childhood or a midlife crisis.

The truth of the matter is that as God renews your youth like the eagles, you actually become more devoted not only to your Heavenly Father, but also to your spouse and family members. Sexual immorality and adultery become the last thing on your mind as God renews your youth.

As we look at the scripture above in Corinthians, we see a fact that many people are not aware of or have never given thought to. Paul tells us that every sin a man commits is outside the physical body, but whoever commits sexual immorality actually sins and does harm to their own physical body or their own physical flesh. This verse should make those thinking of committing sexual sins think, very soberly, before doing so since it will affect their health and wellness of their own physical body.

Let's look at a few more verses that show the outcome and what sexual immorality will produce to those who partake of this destructive sin.

Proverbs 5:8-11 (NKJ) – (Remove your way far from her, and do not go near the door of her house, lest you give your honor to others and your years to the cruel one; lest aliens be filled with your wealth and your labors go to the house of a foreigner; and you mourn at last, when your flesh and your body are consumed.)

Proverbs 6:26 (NKJ) – (For by the means of a harlot a man is reduced to a crust of bread, and an adulteress will prey upon his precious life.)

Proverbs 6:32 (NKJ) – (Whoever commits adultery with a woman lacks understanding; he who does so destroys his own soul.

Proverbs 7:27 (NKJ) – (Her house is the way to hell, descending to the chambers of death)

Even though these verses mention the man, we know that this also works and applies to women as well, for whosoever commits sexual immorality sins against their own flesh and are asking for serious trouble. If you have taken part in sexual immorality or you are contemplating doing so, I urge you to ask God for forgiveness and repent right now. God is just to forgive you as you repent.

Proverbs 28:13 (NKJ) – (He who covers his sins will not prosper, but whoever confesses and forsakes them will have mercy.)

As I mentioned, this chapter is extremely short but needs to be touched upon. As God renews your youth, sexual immorality will be far from your dwelling. As your youth is renewed, I will share one more point in this chapter that may be extremely helpful to you, which is, as God renews your youth physically, mentally, and spiritually, you will certainly feel more vitality, physical energy, and vigor for serving God and life in general.

For example, if you used to play sports and worked out at the gym, but have gotten lazy and stopped doing so, you may and probably will start back with much more physical activity again. This physical energy and vigor will also be noticed by those around you, which will put you in a great place to give a testimonial to the Lord and tell them where all this newly found energy is coming from! Because you will be coming into contact with different people and they will notice your zeal for life, you need to stay aware that this energy should be focused on the things of God and not on the things of the flesh and world.

Keep your focus, and keep your eyes on the prize and off of the things of the world and the flesh. As the verses below tell us.

Job 31:1 (NKJ) – (I have made a covenant with my eyes; why then should I look upon a young woman.)

Psalm 119:37 (NKJ) – (Turn away my eyes from looking at worthless things, and revive me in your way.)

As we look and meditate on the verses above, we understand once again to keep our newly found vigor and vitality on the things of God. The enemy would love to snare you or have you stumble looking at the opposite sex in the wrong way. However, by being aware of this and keeping your eyes on God, and the destiny and assignment he has for you, I know you can avoid any of these potential pitfalls.

As the verse says in Job, he has made a covenant with his eyes, so I would like to suggest to you no matter if you are a man or a woman that you make a covenant with your eyes not to look upon the opposite sex in the wrong way. There is much more work that God has for you to do, and God wants to renew your youth, like the eagles, so that you have the Divine energy to accomplish this task. Like the actual eagles, God will use this keen eyesight to see and stay focused on the things of His kingdom and not be distracted by the things of the world and flesh.

As we close this chapter, I feel led by God to encourage you to ask your Heavenly Father right now, and be in total agreement with Him, that you make a covenant with your eyes to get your focus and keep your focus on His work and the destiny He has for you as you soar higher and higher on eagles wings!

# CHAPTER 15
## IF YOUR EYE IS GOOD

This chapter I will keep short and to the point, however I believe it will give you insight on how God renews our youth like the eagles. This chapter will give you revelation into one of the ways to add years to your life here on earth. We know God is the one who gives us a long life. However, there is biblical wisdom that shows us how God increases our years and vitality, and I will share with you one way this is clearly mentioned in his word. Let's look again at what our Heavenly Father told us about Moses in the book of Deuteronomy.

Deuteronomy 34:7 (NKJ) – (Moses was one hundred and twenty years old when he died. His eyes were not dim nor his natural vigor diminished.)

Let's look at a couple important points of this verse that many people may not see. First of all, we see that Moses died at one hundred twenty years, and his eyesight was still good, and his natural strength was still good. If we look closely, we see that he did not die from some disease or in an unhealthy state, but in great health. His eyesight was good, and he had physical energy and strength. It does not say for sure, but it is safe to say that God simply called Moses home and that his days allotted to Moses had come to an end. Meditate for a moment on this wonderful blessing he was given. He was not sick or in pain, but in great health even at one hundred and twenty years old and God simply called him home. I think that very few people have seen this verse and thought about what I have just shared with you.

Please take the time to meditate upon this powerful yet simple point. The second point I want you to focus on and see is that at one hundred and twenty years old and on his dying day, Moses had good natural physical eyesight. I strongly believe that the reason that Moses' natural eyesight was good is that his spiritual eyesight was good. He had his spiritual eyes set on God and his kingdom, and by doing so, it affected his natural physical eyes, and they were good even on his dying day when God took him home. Where else in God's word do we learn about how our physical bodies are affected by our spiritual eyes? Let's look at this powerful parable in the book of Luke and what Jesus said.

Luke 11:34-36 (NKJ) – (The lamp of the body is the eye. Therefore when your eye is good, your whole body also is full of light. But when your eye is bad, your body also is full of darkness. Therefore take heed that the light which is in you is not darkness. If then your whole body is full of light, having no part dark, the whole body will be full of light, as when the bright shining of a lamp gives you light.)

You can see here that Jesus is saying to us that if our eyes are good, our body is full of light. Please note that he says our body is full of light and not our spirit. It is plain to see that if our eyes are kept on God and his word, our natural physical bodies are affected. By keeping our eyes on Jesus and doing the work of his kingdom, we see that this will give light and health to our physical bodies.

Please reflect for a moment on the fact that if our body is full of light and there is no darkness in our bodies, we are in divine radiant physical health, and no sickness can come upon us. That's right. If our bodies are full of light, no darkness can penetrate, and no illness or disease can come near our physical body or dwelling. How do we make our bodies full of light with no darkness? By seeing who we are in Jesus, and understanding and applying God's word in our lives, and by being active doing the work for the kingdom. Then by doing so, we keep our physical strength and vigor, and our natural eyesight is affected as well as God renews our youth like the eagles. Yes, just like Moses we will keep our physical vitality, and our eyes will not grow dim.

Well, you might be thinking to yourself, I am not Moses nor do I have the calling of Moses. If you think you do not have the calling of Moses, you are exactly right. It is, of course, true that Moses did great things for God and was called the friend of God. However, as you do not have the calling of Moses, Moses also did not have your calling either. God has given you, his child, things to do for his kingdom that Moses did not do and cannot do. You, his precious child, were created for a special unique assignment and destiny that only you can accomplish. Your Heavenly Father created you through his workmanship for good works.

Ephesians 2:10 (NKJ) – (For we are his workmanship, created in Christ Jesus for good works, which God prepared beforehand that we should walk in them.)

As you are reading this book and getting revelation and seeing God's word clearer and clearer, your eyes and vision are getting better and better. As your eyesight becomes keener, your natural body gains more light. As more light comes into your body, any darkness has no choice but to diminish. I believe, at this point, that you are seeing God's word with new vision and clarity which is part of having your youth renewed.

We must have a vision for the things of God, and for the destiny He has given each one of us. For as it is written:

Proverbs 29:18 (NKJ) – (Where there is no revelation, the people cast off restraint; but, happy is he who keeps the law.)

As we look at this verse in Proverbs, we clearly see that if we have no revelation or vision of the things of God, we cast off restraints and will lose track of our destiny. However, we will be happy when we keep the ways of God as our focus. When we keep our vision on God and his ways and wisdom, we are like Moses, whose vision did not fail him, and our bodies are full of light like Jesus mentioned in the parable in the book of Luke. This will put us to work and active for Jesus, and we will experience Divine energy physically, mentally, and spiritually as our youth is renewed.

Yes, if we have this vision for the things of God, we are truly full of light, as Jesus mentioned. Once again, please remember if our bodies are full of light, we will walk in Divine radiant health and have divine physical energy.

Why is this true, you might ask? Two simple reasons with the first reason being this. As you become active doing work for the kingdom of God, you will need Divine physical energy, which our Heavenly Father will provide as he quickens you through the Holy Spirit, which is already in you as a born-again follower of Jesus. This physical energy is needed and will be supplied as you become truly active seeing this revelation.

The second reason is God wants to draw people to you as they see this light and radiance that you can walk in. Jesus makes this very clear, in the book of Luke, that if your eye is good, your whole body is full of light. Jesus tells us in the verse right before this that he wants to fill our bodies full of light. The reason for this is so the world can be drawn to us so that we can be a blessing to them as they see Jesus in us!

So when Jesus sets us on fire with his radiance, he will set us in a position for others to see the light and be drawn to this light.

Luke 11:33 (NKJ) – (No one, when he has lit a lamp, puts it in a secret place or under a basket, but on a lampstand, that those who come in may see the light.)

Just meditate for a moment on this powerful blessing and truth that your Heavenly Father wants to use you, in such a powerful way, and will give you such radiance and light, that people will be drawn towards you! How do we help make this happen? He tells us clearly how in scripture, as we have been discussing. This once again is by keeping our eyes good, which will fill our bodies full of light! I will say it again, and I trust and pray that you will see this powerful revelation with the new Divine vision.

As we keep our eyes upon Jesus, the word of God, and wisdom that the Holy Spirit gives us, our eyes become better and better, and our vision becomes Divine. As we do this, we also start to identify and block out all of the things that the devil and the world try to distract us with in an attempt to take our eyes and vision off the kingdom of God.

As our eyes stay focused on Jesus and his work, we truly soar higher and higher with new improved vision, just like the actual eagles after they finish the molting process. We learn how to fly higher and stay above any storm we may encounter as Jesus lifts us above them and keeps us from being snared or stumbled.

Your Heavenly Father desires and is ready and willing to do this for you, so take heed that your eyes are good so that your whole body will be full of light! It is time for you to be set ablaze with the anointing of God through the Holy Spirit which is in you. God will set you on a lampstand so that people will be drawn to you as they see Jesus in you, and you can be a blessing to them.

Just like Moses, God wants to and will use you in a mighty way, and he will satisfy you with long life, length of days, and peace as you keep your eyes good knowing that it is your Heavenly Father who does this for you as his beloved child in whom he is well pleased!

Proverbs 3:1 (NKJ) – (My son do not forget my law, but let your heart keep my commands, for length of days and long life and peace they will add to you.)

Proverbs 9:11 (NKJ) – (For by me your days will be multiplied, and years of life will be added to you.)

# CHAPTER 16
## SPIRITUAL POWER IN THE PHYSICAL BODY

Judges 14:6 (NKJ) – (and the spirit of the Lord came mightily upon him, and he tore the lion apart as one would have torn apart a young goat, though he had nothing in his hand.)

1 Kings 18:46 (NKJ) – (Then the hand of the Lord came upon Elijah; and he girded up his loins and ran ahead of Ahab to the entrance of Jezreel.)

In this chapter entitled Spiritual Power In The Physical Body, we will look at how the spirit of the Lord can and does empower the children of God as we are doing work for God's kingdom and as we are anointed by God. We will look at a variety of ways this can be done, and we will explore scripture to see examples of this. We will also look at spiritual power in the physical body in the Old Testament in comparison to the New Testament and now.

Let's look at the Old Testament examples first, in the two verses above. As we look at the book of Judges, we see Samson as our first example of someone highly anointed by God. Samson, of course, is also a figure in the Bible who is highly recognized by almost everyone because of his great strength. Samson's great strength came from God, and it is evident from scripture. How did Samson tear the lion apart with his bare hands? Scripture tells us clearly that the spirit of the Lord came upon him mightily.

Let's look at a couple of other examples of Samson's great strength as he was anointed by God, and spiritual power strengthened his physical body.

Judges 15:14-15 (NKJ) – (When he came to Lehi, the Philistines came shouting against him. Then the spirit of the Lord came mightily upon him and the ropes that were on his arms became like flax that is burned with fire and his bonds broke loose from his hands. He found a fresh jawbone of a donkey, reached out his hand and took it, and killed a thousand men with it. Then Samson said, "With the jawbone of a donkey, heaps upon heaps, with the jawbone of a donkey I have slain a thousand men.")

Here is another example of the spirit of the Lord coming upon Samson, and scripture tells us that it came upon him mightily as he killed a thousand men with the jawbone of a donkey. This is one of the most popular Bible stories there is. However, probably most people are familiar with it even though they have never even opened a Bible.

Let's look at one more example of the spirit of the Lord coming upon Samson as he pushed the temple pillars down.

Judges 16:28-30 (NKJ) – (Then Samson called to the Lord saying, "O Lord God, remember me, I pray; strengthen me, I pray, just this once, O God, that I may with one blow take vengeance on the Philistines for my two eyes!" And Samson took hold of the two middle pillars which supported the temple, and he braced himself against them, one on his right and the other on his left. Then Samson said, "Let me die with the Philistines!" And he pushed with all his might, and the temple fell on the lords and all the people who were in it. So the dead that he killed at his death were more than he killed in his life.)

As we look at these three instances and mighty feats of Samson, I want our focus to be on the words that the spirit of the Lord came upon Samson. Understanding this is very important as we move on with this chapter and its teaching. Please meditate on the fact that the spirit of the Lord came upon Samson as he did these great things of physical strength and prowess. Let's turn our focus now to the prophet Elijah who I also showed scripture about at the beginning of this chapter. Once again, let's look at the verse in 1st Kings!

1 Kings 18:46 (NKJ) – (Then the hand of the Lord came upon Elijah; and he girded up his loins and ran ahead of Ahab to the entrance of Jezreel.)

As we look at this verse, we understand that Elijah ran from Mount Carmel to Jezreel and beat Ahab to Jezreel. While doing my research, I found out that the distance from Mount Carmel to Jezreel is about seventeen miles with the route going through a winding mountain road or path. Scripture tells us also that Ahab rode away toward Jezreel which implies he was on his horse and that he started before Elijah, who was on foot and had to physically run the entire route. And after that, scripture tells us that the hand of the Lord came on Elijah, who took off running. However, he ended up running ahead of Ahab, beating him to the destination!

Just like Samson, Elijah had the spirit of the Lord come upon him as he performed this great feat of physical strength and endurance. I could go on and continue adding quite a few instances in the Old Testament that were very impressive feats of physical prowess that were done by warriors and prophets who trusted in God and were fulfilling God's will at the time.

However, I feel that it is important to focus on the New Testament and the present day we live in. I wanted to start with the Old Testament because it gives instances of the spirit of the Lord coming upon those who were basically on a mission for God. This was great news, but what is far greater news is that the spirit of the Lord who came upon these people actually lives inside those today who are born again believers trusting in Jesus Christ. How do I know this to be true?

Romans 8:11 (NKJ) – (But if the Spirit of Him who raised Jesus from the dead dwells in you, he who raised Christ from the dead will also give life to your mortal bodies through his Spirit who dwells in you.)

If this verse does not excite you, I don't know what will. The same spirit that came upon Samson and Elijah who performed those great things actually dwells or lives inside of you as a born-again child of God. As we look at this scripture, we know that this spirit is the same spirit who not only raised Jesus from the dead, but this same spirit dwells or stays within you! Dwell means to stay within you, so wherever you go he goes. In the Old Testament this spirit once again had to come upon the person, but now he stays within you at all times. Knowing this, we need to right now give thanks to the Lord as it is written below!

Psalm 150:2 (NKJ) – (Praise him for his mighty acts; praise him according to his excellent greatness;)

As we look again at the verse in Romans, we also see that the spirit of God who dwells in us will also give life and strength to our mortal or physical bodies. Since this book is about renewing your youth like the eagles, and this chapter is about spiritual power in the physical body, we will focus on the physical aspect right now.

The Holy Spirit will surely give us life, power, and anointing in our physical bodies as we move forward doing work for the kingdom of God. As we look deeper into this, let's view a couple of examples of this in the New Testament, where the spirit of the Lord dwelled within the person.

One powerful example of spiritual power in the physical body was Paul in the book of Acts, where the bite of a viper had no effect on him.

Acts 28:3-5 (NKJ) – (But when Paul had gathered a bundle of sticks and laid them on the fire, a viper came out because of the heat and fastened to his hand; so when the natives saw the creature hanging from his hand, they said to one another, no doubt this man is a murderer, whom though he has escaped the sea, yet justice does not allow him to live; but he shook off the creature into the fire and suffered no harm.)

As we can see, the bite of the poison viper had no effect upon Paul. Why? Because he was busy doing God's work, and the same spirit that raised Jesus from the dead dwelled within him. THE SAME WAY HE DOES WITH YOU AS A CHILD OF GOD!

You have the same power in you because the Spirit gives you life and quickens your physical body to accomplish the destiny God has for you. Yes, that's right, as you move forward to do the work of God's kingdom you are with all might physically, as well as mentally, and spiritually.

Colossians 1:11 (NKJ) – (Strengthened with all might according to his glorious power, with all patience and longsuffering with joy.)

Philippians 4:13 (NKJ) – (I can do all things through Christ who strengthens me.)

Yes, you can do all things through Christ who strengthens you, and this means physically as well, as it pertains to the work of God. Doing the work of God requires physical energy and strength in your physical body, and it is important to understand that the spirit of God within you gives you this physical strength to do God's work as he renews your youth like the eagles. He supplies you with all the power necessary and power over every obstacle or roadblock of the enemy.

Luke 10:19 (NKJ) – (Behold I give you authority to trample upon serpents and scorpions and over all the power of the enemy and nothing shall by any means hurt you.)

Psalm 91:13 (NKJ) – (You shall tread upon the lion and the cobra. The young lion and the serpent you shall trample underfoot.)

Look also at the verse below as it also pertains to the power, physically within you, as you are doing the work for the kingdom of God.

Mark 16:17 (NKJ) – (They will take up serpents; and if they drink anything deadly, it will by no means hurt them; they will lay hands on the sick, and they will recover.)

Please look closely at the verse above and meditate on it, and God will give you the revelation of the power that is already within you through the Holy Spirit who GIVES YOU LIFE!

A simple example of this was Paul's handkerchief or prayer cloth.

Acts 19:12 (NKJ) – (So that even handkerchief's or aprons were brought from his body to the sick and the disease left them, and the evil spirits went out of them.)

Another example of this powerful life-giving anointing of the Holy Spirit within one's body is listed below concerning the apostle Peter.

Acts 5:15 (NKJ) – (So that they brought the sick out into the streets and laid them on beds and couches, that at least the shadow of Peter passing by might fall on some of them.)

As you can see, there was enough anointing in Paul's physical body, through the spirit that lived within him, that the apron or handkerchief that was against his physical body could physically heal those touched by it. This was because of the anointing of the Holy Spirit. I could continue giving examples of people from the Bible who had and also used this spiritual power in their physical bodies to do the work of the Lord.

However, let's turn the focus to this present day and how we, as God's children, can tap into this power and use it in our work for the kingdom. As I mentioned before, we have been looking at how God renews our youth, like the eagles in three ways, with all three ways being yoked together. As we look further, the physical anointing, which comes upon us and is needed as we walk in Divine health and physical energy, is given to us to accomplish the work God has for us.

Simply understand that this physical strength and energy are for you as believers, and God's word has a lot to say about it. Let's look at God's will for your physical health. This should clear up any confusion you may have regarding God's will on this benefit you have as a child of God!

3 John 2 (NKJ) – (Beloved I wish above all things that you prosper and be in health just as your soul prospers.)

Your Heavenly Father is telling you in the above verse that ABOVE ALL THINGS, HIS WILL IS FOR YOU TO PROSPER AND BE IN HEALTH JUST AS YOUR SOUL PROSPERS!

With this in mind, let me share some verses in God's word that speak of you being in divine health and having youthful energy. These verses are just a handful. There are literally hundreds I could have chosen. These verses are also those that are clearly showing the health and youthfulness you can walk in even though you may not have ever seen them in this light before now, as I will point out to you.

Psalm 92:12 (NKJ) – (The righteous shall flourish like a palm tree, he shall grow like a cedar in Lebanon.)

As you meditate on the above verse, knowing that you are righteous in Jesus, and now think just how healthy a palm tree is and how it flourishes! Now think how strong and sturdy a cedar tree is and how it grows in strength and beauty! This is purely Divine health and strength, and God is clearly saying to you that you are like the flourishing palm tree and the sturdy cedar tree. And, it is high time we start thanking him for this!

Psalm 1:3 (NKJ) – (He shall be like a tree planted by the rivers of water, that brings forth its fruit in season and whose leaf also shall not wither; and whatever he does shall prosper.)

As we meditate on the above verse, again, we see that we flourish in all our ways, including our physical health and vitality. Notice that our health here is divine because our leaf will not wither, and whatever we do shall prosper. Let's look at a very similar verse in the book of Jeremiah that talks about how we are to flourish and that our leaf will be green and healthy.

Jeremiah 17:8 (NKJ) – (For he shall be like a tree planted by the waters, which spreads out its roots by the river, and will not fear when heat comes; but its leaf will be green, and will not be anxious in the year of drought, nor will cease from yielding fruit.)

Proverbs 11:28 (NKJ) – (But the righteous will flourish like the foliage.)

Isaiah 58:11 (NKJ) – (The Lord will continually guide you, and satisfy your soul in drought, and strengthen your bones; you shall be like a watered garden, and like a spring of water, whose waters do not fail.)

As we look at these verses, we see that when we trust and follow the Lord, we are likened to a flourishing tree, plant, bush, or garden, which is watered and planted in good soil. It is important to understand that the good soil we need to be planted in … is the Lord!

Psalm 92:13 (NKJ) – (Those who are planted in the house of the Lord, shall flourish in the courts of our Lord.)

Let's look closely at the verse below and how it pertains to our physical health.

Psalm 91:10 (NKJ) – (No evil shall befall you, nor shall any plague come near your dwelling.)

The Lord is telling us here, in this powerful verse, that first of all no evil will befall us when we trust in Him and dwell with Him. Then he tells us that no plague will come near our dwelling. You might ask, what is our dwelling? Well, our natural house or where we reside is our dwelling, but also, our physical body is our dwelling or temple and where the Holy Spirit dwells.

1 Corinthians 3:16 (NKJ) – (Do you not know that you are the temple of God and that the spirit of God dwells in you.)

2 Timothy 1:14 (NKJ) – (Which was committed to you, kept by the Holy Spirit who dwells in you.)

God is telling us clearly that no plague or sickness will come near our dwelling, our physical body, when we trust and dwell in Jesus! How does he do this, you might ask? Well, one way is listed in Psalm 91 right after the verse we are discussing.

Psalm 91:11 (NKJ) – (For he shall give his angels charge over you, to keep you in all your ways.)

God's mighty angels will keep us in all our ways, and one of these ways is, of course, the health and wellbeing of our natural physical body, which is the temple or dwelling place of the Holy Spirit. This should give you a powerful revelation and assurance that our Heavenly Father is watching over our physical bodies which actually belong to him!

Let's also look at some scriptures in which our Heavenly Father promises us a long healthy life.

Psalm 91:16 (NKJ) – (With long life I will satisfy him, and show him my salvation.)

Proverbs 3:1-2 (NKJ) – (My son, do not forget my law, but let your heart keep my commands; for length of days and long life and peace they will add to you.)

Proverbs 4:10 (NKJ) – (Hear my son and receive my sayings, and the years of your life will be many.)

Proverbs 9:11 (NKJ) – (For by me your days will be multiplied, and years of life will be added to you.)

Psalm 92:14-15 (NKJ) – (They shall still bear fruit in old age; they shall be fresh and flourishing. To declare that the Lord is upright; he is my rock and there is no unrighteousness in him.)

As we look at these verses, we can clearly see that our Heavenly Father wants to give us a long, healthy life and that a long, healthy life is a promise to his children. We can clearly see that a long healthy life is obtainable and will happen if we follow the Lord trusting in him and also understanding that this is a benefit we have as a child of God. I have also seen that the more active we are for the kingdom of God the more physically vibrant we become as God renews our youth!

As we close this chapter on spiritual power in the physical body, let's look to one more scripture regarding Moses.

Deuteronomy 34:7 (NKJ) – (Moses was one hundred and twenty years old when he died. His eyes were not dim nor his natural vigor diminished.)

As we focus on the above verse about Moses, we see that he had good eyesight and kept his physical vigor and strength up to his dying day at the age of 120 years. This goes to show us that trusting in God, being active in the work of his kingdom, and also understanding the benefit we have as children of God is what renews our youth like the eagles. It is also vitally important to highly understand the point I made earlier. We have a much better covenant than they had in the Old Testament.

As I mentioned earlier, the spirit of the Lord would have to come upon the people of that day. But now, through the cross and the blood of Jesus, the spirit of the Lord lives inside us and does not have to come upon us anymore, because he is always upon us and within us! Let's look again at the verse in Romans.

Romans 8:11 (NKJ) – (But if the spirit of him who raised Jesus from the dead dwells in you, he who raised Christ from the dead will also give life to your mortal bodies through his Spirit who dwells in you.)

I will tell you briefly about one of my own experiences of spiritual power in the physical body. Even though the Holy Spirit is always at work within us and his power manifests itself in a variety of ways, this example is a true display of physical strength and vigor with God getting all the glory. As I will give you a short overview, however, if you are interested in a longer version, I wrote an entire chapter on this example in my book, The Stone and the Sling.

A couple of years ago, in the town of Fairmont, North Carolina, Kirk Nobles and I pulled a semi-truck, weighing slightly over forty thousand pounds, the distance of one full mile using only our physical strength for a world record. We were able to pull the truck the one-mile distance in only fifty minutes and fifty-four seconds. The first three-quarters of a mile was flat and the last quarter of a mile had a slight upgrade.

The one-mile pull was very hard, and I can say without a doubt that the Holy Spirit strengthened and quickened our physical bodies. We did this record feat giving all the glory to the Lord, and the record was covered by several magazines, and Duke University's human performance lab did tests on me throughout the pulling. They said my statistics on the pulling were world-class, to say the least even though I was in my fifties.

I tell you this story not to impress you, but to impress upon you that God has renewed my youth like the eagles, and he will do the same for you as this is one of your benefits!

Psalm 103:5 (NKJ) – (He puts good things in your mouth, so that your youth is renewed like the eagles.)

# CHAPTER 17
## THE YOUTHFUL SPIRIT

Job 33:25 (NIV) – (Let their flesh be renewed like a child's; let them be restored as in the days of their youth.)

In this chapter, we will look at some examples of what you will experience as God renews your youth like the eagles. I mentioned earlier that God does this physically, mentally, and spiritually. It is important to understand that the physical and mental renewing follow the spiritual, and it must start with the spiritual as you get closer to God and feel His presence.

As we truly seek God and his kingdom, looking at everything that Jesus purchased on the cross for us, we can truly trust that everything else will be added!

Matthew 6:33 (NIV) – (But seek first his kingdom and his righteousness and all these things will be given to you as well.)

Yes, seek first the kingdom of God, and what will follow? All else will follow including YOUR physical and mental renewing! I am 60 years old now and have noticed that the more I seek the Lord and have a thirst for his word and wisdom the more zeal I have experienced and continue to experience.

This zeal for the Lord quickly creates more physical energy and more mental clarity! This zeal for God's kingdom keeps your focus on the Lord and his kingdom. Therefore, you don't get overly caught up in the things of this world but on His kingdom instead.

Proverbs 23:17-18 (NKJ) – (Do not let your heart envy sinners, but be zealous for the fear of the Lord all day; For surely there is a hereafter and your hope will not be cut off.)

You may be thinking this sounds good, but I have a life, a job, and a family. This is true, of course, and no one understands this more than God because He gave you those things and created you. However, as you do this, you begin to see everything as an opportunity to serve God and His kingdom! That's right, even your workplace becomes a ministry, and the Lord will show you certain opportunities to make a difference. You are doing this for the Lord and His kingdom, and He will reward you, and all else will be added as you do everything heartily unto the Lord.

Colossians 3:23-24 (NKJ) – (And whatever you do, do it heartily, as to the Lord and not to men, knowing that from the Lord you will receive the reward of the inheritance: for you serve the Lord Christ.)

Trust me, you can make a huge difference in your center of influence that you live in, work in, and walk-in, as God renews your youth His way. As you seek the Lord and press into Him and be diligent, you will start the renewing process, and you will soon become zealous for the things of the Lord. You will be seeking the kingdom first, and you will feel His love, power, and presence working in you.

Colossians 1:29 (NKJ) – (To this end I also labor, striving according to His working which works in me mightily.)

Many of you remember back when you first made Jesus Lord and Savior and were saved. You probably felt that excitement and zeal, but little by little you lost the zeal. This may happen due to life's circumstances that pulled your vision off Jesus. If this is true, as it has been with many of us, we have lost our zeal for our first love, which is Jesus.

The great news is God wants to renew us back to those days, which is our youth. You may be saying that you feel bad that you lost this initial zeal for Jesus because of life's difficulties or circumstances. However, what does the word renew mean? It means you have lost something, but now it gets renewed and refreshed.

You may be saying this sounds great, but what about my circumstances? Well let's think about the eagle that flies above the storm using the wind to its advantage. This storm that the eagle faces is like your circumstances, which God will lift YOU above! As God renews your youth and raises you above your circumstances, these difficulties may completely vanish, or as he lifts you above them you may not even notice them anymore.

Also, if we are diligent and continue to trust in the Lord, these difficulties and circumstances have a strong promotion behind them! For example, without Goliath, there would not have been such a great promotion for David!

Our job is to trust in the Lord and diligently keep seeking him with a youthful, trusting spirit just like a child trusts its mother.

Psalm 131:1-2 (NKJ) – (Neither do I concern myself with great matters, nor with things too profound for me. Surely I have calmed and quieted my soul like a weaned child with his mother; Like a weaned child is my soul within me.)

We have looked at the importance of looking and returning to the Lord with our spiritual eyes open and trusting in him with a youthful childlike spirit. As we do this, our youth starts to renew, and our mind and body follow.

Now let's look at how our mental clarity is renewed as well. I truly believe our mental clarity and eyes and ears start to see and hear what God is saying to us as He shows us our assignments, our personal destiny, and His will for our lives.

Romans 12:2 (NIV) – (Do not conform to the pattern of this world, but be transformed by the renewing of your mind. Then you will be able to test and approve what God's will is – his good, pleasing and perfect will.)

As you seek the Lord and commit your works to him, he will change and renew your mind and establish your thoughts.

Proverbs 16:3 (NKJ) – (Commit your works to the Lord, and your thoughts will be established.)

It becomes very exciting as your youth gets renewed, and God starts talking to you and shows you the different things that he has for you. He greatly wants you to walk in all the blessings Jesus purchased for you on the cross. You may be used to hearing God's voice, but you may be thinking that you're not used to hearing His voice, and you may not even know if you can.

Let me show you a few examples in scripture of how God talks to His children. Remember also that God may show you a picture or vision in your mind or even in a dream. This is why it is important to listen to and study God's word. We must have spiritual eyes to see and spiritual ears to hear.

Proverbs 20:12 (NKJ) – (The hearing ear and the seeing eye. The Lord has made them both.

Like I mentioned, God can show you a certain picture or vision that aligns itself with His written word or aligns itself with a thought you have been pondering. This can be true especially if the thought or vision is to help others by telling them about Jesus or to encourage them in the Lord.

Numbers 12:6 (NIV) – (Then he said, "Hear my words; If there is a prophet among you, I, the Lord will make myself known to him in a vision: I speak to him in dreams.")

Amos 3:7 (NKJ) – (Surely the Lord God does nothing unless he reveals his secret to his servants the prophets.)

One way I have heard from the Lord, powerfully, was by speaking the below verse and then thanking the Lord for answering me. Jeremiah 33:3 (NKJ) – (Call to me, and I will answer you and show you great and mighty things, which you do not know.)

This is a powerful verse, and God makes it clear and simple! Call on Him, He will answer you and show you great and mighty things you do not know! I urge you to follow His simple instructions and then thank Him for answering you while you wait expectantly for his answer!

Psalm 5:3 (NIV) – (In the morning, Lord, you hear my voice; In the morning I lay my requests before you and wait expectantly.)

The Lord wants to hear from you, and He greatly desires to teach and show you great and mighty things. You are also speaking His word, following His instructions, and He watches over His word to perform it!

Jeremiah 1:12 (NKJ) – (Then the Lord said to me, "You have seen well, for I am ready to perform My word.")

As you listen to the Lord, and He speaks to you and reveals great and mighty things to you, you will enter closer and closer to Him feeling His presence. This is renewing and refreshing, and you will want more and more of His presence as you dwell and abide with Him!

As He speaks to you and reveals great things and plans He has for your life, be sure to write His words and vision down on a tablet.

Habakkuk 2:1-3 (NKJ) – (I will stand my watch and set myself on the rampart and watch to see what I will answer when I am reproved. Then the Lord answered me and said; "Write the vision and make it plain on tablets, that he may run who reads it. For the vision is yet for an appointed time; But, in the end it will speak and it will not lie. Though it tarries, wait for it Because it will surely come, it will not tarry.")

As you see in the verses above, it is important to write down the special visions and words God speaks to you and trust in Him waiting patiently as He brings it to pass. Doing this will breathe new life and excitement back into you. It will help renew your mind as you trust in the Lord with simple youthful childlike faith, which is part of renewing your youth! Trust in the Lord, and the dreams He has planted in your heart will surely come to pass.

Psalm 37:5 (NKJ) – (Commit your way to the Lord, trust also in him and he shall bring it to pass.)

I have shown you how God starts to renew you spiritually and mentally. Now I will touch on a few things you may notice physically. I am going to keep this short because I have written in-depth about the physical changes in some of the other chapters.

There are countless things you may experience, but I am sure you will experience a new-found strength renewing your physical energy. This is because of the new excitement and zeal you have for the things of God. The Lord has many things for you to do for His kingdom, and He will supply the physical strength and energy you need to do this. He also wants those you come into contact with to notice your newly found energy so you can tell them the reason. It will be a great testimonial.

This will open new doors for you to tell people about Jesus, and all He has done for you, and that He wants to do the same for them! You may also notice you wake up easier and earlier in the morning. You will laugh more and have a much more joyful spirit about yourself. You may notice yourself watching and looking at clouds in the sky or watching ants work in the dirt or notice flowers and trees more.

These types of things become much more natural as God renews your youth physically. People may notice you actually look younger, and your eyes look clearer as you walk in this benefit. The list goes on and on as God renews your youth.

Personally, one of the things I noticed was a new love for walking barefoot on the trails and in the woods and doing yard work completely barefoot. Many things that you quit doing because you felt too old may come back, and you may start doing them again. This is God blessing you, so ENJOY!

Psalm 37:4 (NKJ) – Delight yourself in the Lord and he shall give you the desires of your heart.)

# CHAPTER 18
## FLOOR SITTING/GROUND SLEEPING

In this chapter, I will show you one of the natural ways to help renew your youth. In fact, what we will look at is something that pretty much all children do naturally. However, most adults have gotten away from doing. I will show you a couple of simple ways to restore your hip mobility, which should also help you relieve any back discomfort you may be experiencing.

As we get older, we tend to lose hip mobility, which in return affects our general mobility. One of the major causes of this decreased mobility is too much sitting in traditional chairs, which shortens our hip flexors and also numbs our glute muscles, which keep them from activating the way they should.

You may be thinking, this is interesting, but what does this have to do with renewing your youth God's way? Well, there is a simple answer, and that is the people of biblical times and even in some regions today did not or do not sit in traditional chairs, but instead, when they were not standing to work, they sat on the floor or ground. That's right, even though we don't think about it much Moses, Samson, the apostle Paul, the apostle Peter, and Jesus himself, generally sat and rested on the floor on a mat or outside on the grass or dirt on the ground.

John 6:10 (NIV) – (Jesus said, have the people sit down, There was plenty of grass in that place and they sat down, about five thousand men were there.)

It was certainly standard practice to sit on the ground or floor in those days, which kept their hips and spine more mobile and supple. Research has shown there are more back and hip issues today than ever before and much of this is from sitting on chairs. We also know that sitting on the floor helps keep us more supple and mobile. In fact, I have personally found that going back to floor sitting can help restore mobility in my hips, which in return helps restore my mobility in general.

Just think back to the days when you were a child, where did you usually sit? You sat on the floor to watch television, play games, or even to simply rest and relax. Did you feel more flexible then? Well this is one of the reasons why, as you kept your hips more supple.

Research has found that even in today's times, cultures who do more floor sitting and living report far less hip and back issues than modern culture who sit more in traditional chairs! So let's think back again to biblical times when Jesus sat on the ground, not traditional chairs, and we can see why this is good for us and certainly can help restore and renew our mobility in our hips, which also helps renew our mobility in general!

You may be thinking that sitting on the floor sounds uncomfortable or undignified, and it's not for you. Well, floor sitting can be a little uncomfortable at first but, the rewards can be remarkable and life-changing as you renew your hip mobility!

I felt strongly prompted by the Lord to add this chapter even though I knew there would be quite a few readers who would not try floor sitting. However, here is a simple challenge I have for you. Simply try sitting on the floor inside or the ground outside for 15 minutes each day. After you try this a bit, you may even find you want to extend your duration of time sitting on the ground due to the renewing of your hip mobility and increased mobility in general!

Below are five easy and simple positions to try out on the floor. You can sit in one position for a while or simply move from one position to another after a couple of minutes in one position. You may feel fairly comfortable in one position but uncomfortable in another. Simply play around and see what works best for you. All five positions will help renew your hip flexors over time.

It's important to keep your spine straight in these positions and to follow the instructions with each position. Last but not least, be sure to breathe normally and relax, as these positions are good for you! Have fun and let your inner child come out while you are in these positions as God renews your youth!

However, if any of these positions feel more than a bit uncomfortable and cause you any pain, or if you have an existing injury don't push yourself and be sure to speak to your health care provider before you continue.

The images below in the sitting positions are of Dani Almeyda of Original Strength. Original Strength is a system of natural God-given movements created by Tim Anderson which are designed to reset the body and restore mobility. I highly recommend you look at Tim's website which is Original Strength.net

Position 1 – The Long Sit – Follow theses image closely and be sure to relax and keep a straight neutral spine.

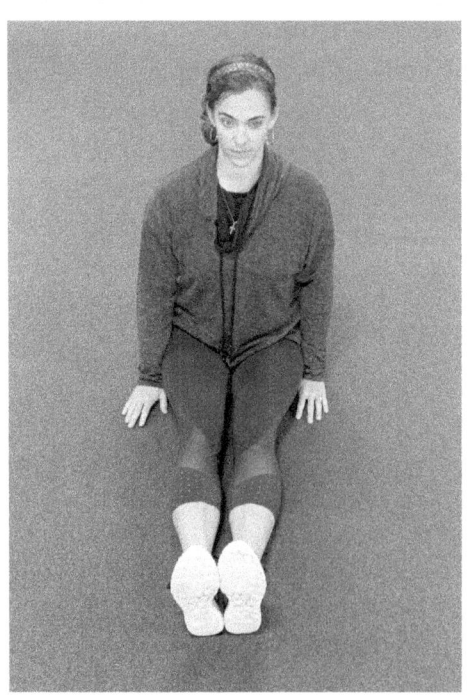

Position 2 – Cross-Legged – Follow the image closely and be sure and relax and keep a straight neutral spine.

Position 3 – Side Saddle – Follow the image closely and be sure and relax and keep a straight neutral spine.

Position 4 – Knees Up – Follow these images closely and be sure and relax and keep a straight neutral spine.

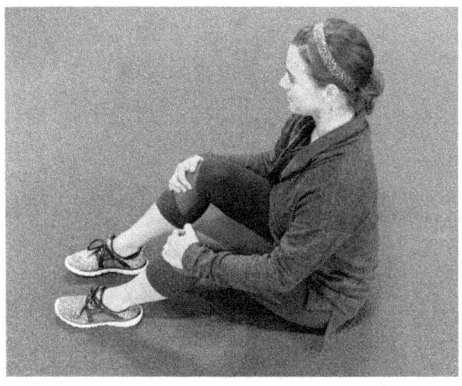

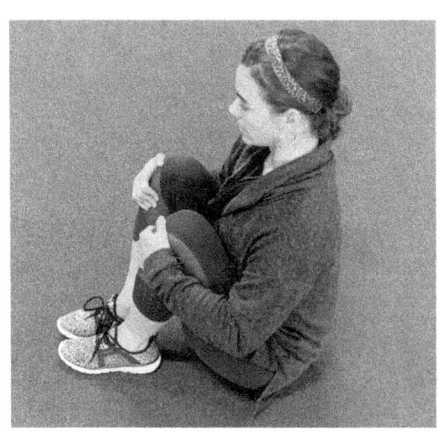

Position 5 – Cobra Position – Follow the images closely and only extend your back to where you are comfortable. As you improve you can gradually arch your back higher.

In the first 4 floor positions you may sit on a pillow or pad to get into the proper position if this helps and makes you more comfortable.

These five floor sitting/resting positions are probably the easiest to adapt to even though there are many more ways and variations to sit and rest on the floor. Try these and progress over time, and your hips and mobility will thank you as they experience a form of natural youthful renewing!

Remember, this is how God created man to relax and rest and is part of renewing your youth, God's way, which is one of YOUR benefits as a follower of Jesus!

In this chapter, I also want to briefly mention sleeping on the floor or ground which was something that everyone did in ancient times and some still do in many countries today. In the Bible it mentions people using mats to lie and sleep on. We also know that when man was created there were no modern-day beds or pillows at all but only the ground to sleep on.

We also know that countries who still sleep on the ground report far less back pain as well as a better night's sleep! Many people with back discomfort report that sleeping on the ground helps their back discomfort as their spine stays in better alignment.

It is not actually the floor itself that helps them but a harder surface than today's mattresses gives them. Someone can simply lay on the floor, with a mat, like they did in biblical times, or you can have a bed off the ground with, for example, a plywood plank with a mat or two over the plank.

Something like a yoga mat or slightly thicker will give you a bit of padding but still give you a harder surface to keep your spine aligned and from sagging like with a regular mattress. Also, by using a regular bed off the ground you can avoid dust on the ground.

Like the floor sitting we discussed, sleeping on the ground or hard surface has some benefits, and if anyone doubts this they simply need to look back at how early man slept and how healthy they were in general. Their bones and joints were good, and they were strong and supple.

I suggest that you try some floor sitting and ground sleeping, which was how God created us to sit and rest. These once again are natural God-given physical ways that God can renew your youth!

# CHAPTER 19
## YOUTH STEALERS

Ephesians 4:31-32 (NKJ) – (Let all bitterness, wrath, anger, clamor and evil speaking be put away from you, with all malice and be kind to one another, tenderhearted, forgiving one another, even as God in Christ forgave you.)

As this book is about renewing our youth, God's way, and the powerful benefit He has given us to be able to do this through Jesus, this book would not be complete without this chapter.

As you can see, from the chapter title above, this chapter is called The Youth Stealers. I believe there is nothing that can keep us from experiencing the benefit of renewed youth more than lack of forgiveness. In fact, I believe it can also age us before our time and shorten our days.

Even though this chapter is short and to the point, it is my prayer and hope that you, by the end of this chapter, will be able to get rid of any unforgiveness that is weighing you down and holding you back from experiencing what Jesus purchased for you on the cross.

Like the eagles that get weighed down and go through the molting process to soar higher, we need to get rid of the baggage weighing us down so we can truly soar and fulfill our destiny in Jesus! Let me share a few scriptures with you, and I ask that you meditate closely on them to see if you need to get rid of any excess baggage weighing you down from soaring like the eagles.

Matthew 18:21-22 (NIV) – (Then Peter came to Jesus and asked, "Lord, how many times shall I forgive my brother when he sins against me? Up to seven times?" Jesus answered, "I tell you, not seven times, but seventy-seven times.")

Hebrews 12:15 (NKJ) – (See to it that no one comes short of the grace of God; that no root of bitterness springing up causes trouble and by it many be defiled.)

Matthew 6:14-15 (NKJ) – (For if you forgive other people when they sin against you, your Heavenly Father will also forgive you. But, if you do not forgive others their sins, your Father will not forgive your sins.)

As we look at these verses, we can understand that not forgiving can certainly weigh us down, and any lack of forgiveness or bitterness does not come from God and above. Instead that comes from the devil, our adversary, to hinder and steal from us!

James 3:14-18 (NKJ) – (But if you have bitter envy and self-seeking in your hearts, do not boast and lie against truth. This wisdom does not come from above, but is earthly, sensual, and demonic. For where envy and self-seeking exist, confusion and every evil thing are there. But, the wisdom that is from above is first pure, then peaceable, gentle, willing to yield, full of mercy and good fruits, without partiality and without hypocrisy. Now the fruit of righteousness is sown in peace.)

Now is the time that we do not let the devil steal from us anymore, so we can walk in God's fullness and experience true peace and joy and help others find and experience peace and joy through the forgiveness of Jesus! Please meditate for a moment on what Jesus did on the cross for you. He died and shed his blood so you could have your sins forgiven and have everlasting life with Him in heaven.

You can see how important forgiveness is and why you must forgive others as he forgave YOU! With this being said, you can see why the thief, the devil, fights so hard against forgiveness and why he wants you to hold onto unforgiveness of others, which holds you back and steals your peace and joy. Please understand that Jesus is here to give you life and life more abundantly!

John 10:10 (NKJ) – (The thief does not come except to steal, and to kill, and to destroy. I have come that they may have life, and that they may have it more abundantly.)

Isn't it time you receive and walk in this life, now? Claim the abundance that Jesus already purchased for you on the cross! You can do this right now by submitting to God and resisting the devil who tries to get you to hold onto unforgiveness.

James 4:7 (NKJ) – (Therefore submit to God. Resist the devil and he will flee from you.)

Please understand that it is the adversary, who is your enemy and the one who is trying to steal from you, not the people around you. People are responsible and accountable for their actions however, you must let go and forgive them, which releases you into God's peace and joy!

God clearly tells us that He will avenge, and He will contend with those who contend with you!

Romans 12:19 (NKJ) – (Dearly beloved, avenge not yourselves, but rather give place unto wrath for it is written, vengeance is mine; I will repay, saith the Lord.)

Isaiah 49:25 (NKJ) – (Even the captives of the mighty shall be taken away, and prey of the terrible be delivered; for I will contend with him who contends with you and I will save your children.)

As these verses saturate into your spirit, let's right now pray and release any unforgiveness or bitterness into the open arms of Jesus!

(Heavenly Father, I come in the name of Jesus, and I release my unforgiveness and bitterness to you. And, I ask for your forgiveness for this, and I repent that I have carried this in my heart. Thank you, Jesus, for taking this burden from me and forgiving me in your name Jesus. Amen!

Congratulations, and praise the Lord for YOUR BREAKTHROUGH! As you walk in forgiveness you will feel the weight lift off your shoulders and you will start to feel more peace and joy in the Lord! This peace and joy in your heart will renew everything including your physical body.

Proverbs 14:30 (NIV) – (A heart at peace gives life to the body.)

As we close this short but crucial chapter, be diligent in keeping any kind of lack of forgiveness or bitterness from creeping back in. Keep your eyes on Jesus and be zealous for Him and His kingdom works. As you do this, your old lack of forgiveness and bitterness will be like water passing under the bridge that never returns!

Job 11:16 (NIV) – (You will surely forget your misery; It will be like waters gone by.)

# CHAPTER 20
## THE SUN SHALL NOT SMITE YOU

Psalm 121:6 (NKJ) – (The sun shall not smite you by day, nor the moon by night.)

I felt extremely led to write this chapter even though it is short. God created the sun to sustain life and for the entire earth's benefit, including us! However, the sun often strikes fear into many people with much of the fear coming from the thought of skin cancer. Whether you believe that the sun causes skin cancer or not we will not get into that, and if you look at the research you will find a lot of mixed thoughts on the matter.

What I would like to speak to you about in this chapter is what God says about the sun, His protection, and also the importance of Vitamin D for your physical health. Let's look first at a verse in Psalm about the sun and what it does on the earth!

Psalm 19:5-6 (NKJ) – (Which is like a bridegroom coming out of his chamber and rejoices like a strong man to run its race. Its rising is from one end to the other end; and there is nothing hidden from its heat.)

This verse shows how magnificent the sun is and tells us it rises from one end of heaven and runs its course to the other end! The Lord has complete control over the sun and your safety and protection if you will let him.

A while back, at the beach, as I was watching people frantically put on sunscreen in such a hurry, as if they would literally perish if they took even a few more seconds to apply the sunscreen. I started thinking about this and also how so many well-meaning dermatologists strike fear into people about the thought of skin cancer and the sun. As I meditated on this, I thought how God could have possibly created something that we could not even be outside in because it could harm us so easily. Then, I realized he could not!

In fact, the sun's rays help keep us healthy and joyful. Science has taught us that if our vitamin D blood levels are over 50 and between 50 – 80 ng.ml, our bodies can ward off most of the deadly diseases of today like cancer and heart disease. When our vitamin D levels are deficient we are more prone to such things.

As many of you know, even though you take vitamin D supplements to raise your levels, the natural way is from the sun. God does not make mistakes, and the sun being above you and shining its rays on you is no mistake as it helps keep you healthy and joyful.

I truly believe that as the sun shines down with its rays on you, God supplies a spiritual covering or cloud that protects you from any damage from the sun or anything else. Even though a nice cloud feels good on a hot sunny day, this is no natural cloud but spiritual shade that protects you.

Let's look back as the Israelites were in the desert sun and heat. Did they use number 50 sunscreen to protect them from the sun? No, God supplied them with divine protection overhead from a cloud. Even though this cloud could be seen in the sky, it was no ordinary cloud but, spiritual shade sent from God almighty!

Exodus 40:38 (NKJ) – (For the cloud of the Lord was above the tabernacle by day and fire was over it by night, in the sight of all the house of Israel throughout all their journeys.)

Psalm 105:39 (NKJ) – (He spread a cloud for a covering and fire to give light in the night.)

We can see that God supplied the cloud to cover them from not only the desert sun but to also guide them through their journeys! We must understand that a little bit of sunlight is good for us and supplied by God. We must learn to believe and operate in faith, not in fear, as God renews our youth like the eagles. Just like the real eagle goes through the molting process and gets rid of things weighing it down, we must get rid of fear, unforgiveness, bitterness, envy, etc., so we can soar higher and be all God created us to be.

Enjoy life and the sun's rays without fear as God says in Isaiah, he will satisfy your needs in a sun-scorched land.

Isaiah 58:11 (NIV) – (The Lord will guide you always; he will satisfy your needs in a sun-scorched land.)

As the name of this chapter says, the sun will not smite you. Let's look at the verse below and see why the sun won't smite you!

Psalm 121:5-6 (KJV) (The Lord is your keeper; the Lord is your shade at your right hand. The sun shall not smite thee by day nor the moon by night.)

We can clearly see that if you have made Jesus Lord and Savior and trust in his word and promise the sun will not smite or harm you. Why? The Lord is your shade! As we look closely with our spiritual eyes, we can see the protection of the Lord all through his word and around us as we go through our daily activities.

As I mentioned at the beginning of this chapter, I will keep this one short and to the point. However, I do encourage you to enjoy the sunshine the Lord has given YOU as it will enhance your overall health greatly. I also encourage you to look solely to the Lord for your provision and safety as he cares for you and has provided all the shade and protection you will ever need under the shadow of his wings!

Psalm 17:8 (NKJ) – (Keep me as the apple of your eye; hide me under the shadow of your wings.)

Ruth 2:12 (NKJ) – (The Lord repay your work and a full reward given you by the Lord God of Israel, under whose wings you have come for refuge.)

Psalm 57:1 (NKJ) – (For my soul trusts in you; and in the shadow of your wings I will make my refuge, until these calamities have passed by.)

Psalm 91:1 (NKJ) – (He who dwells in the secret place of the most high shall abide under the shadow of the almighty.)

# CHAPTER 21
## THIRST NO MORE

John 4:13-14 (NKJ) – (Jesus answered and said to her, whoever drinks of this water will thirst again, but whoever drinks of the water that I shall give him will never thirst. But the water that I shall give him will become in him a fountain of water springing up into everlasting life.)

In this chapter, we will look at the importance of being properly hydrated and drinking enough water. I know that saying and talking about this sounds so elementary even though it is so crucial. Everyone knows to drink plenty of water and to stay hydrated. However, very few actually do.

This chapter will touch on the importance of physical hydration and doing it as well as what God says about our spiritual hydration which is even more important. As we look at our physical hydration, first let me point you to a few scriptures that show the importance of water and how it revives and energizes us.

Let's look first at how Samson was totally revived from drinking the water that God supplied him. This example is in the book of Judges, where Samson just killed one thousand Philistines with the jawbone of a donkey.

Judges 15:18-19 (NIV) – (Then he became very thirsty; so he cried out to the Lord and said, "You have given this great deliverance by thy hand of your servant; and now I die of thirst and fall into the hand of the uncircumcised?" So God split the hollow place that is in Lehi and water came out and he drank; and his strength returned and he revived.)

As we see in these verses, Samson was dehydrated and thirsty, but right after he received and drank the water God supplied to him, he revived and his strength returned. This is a very simple, but powerful, message of how water and being hydrated sustains us and keeps us healthy and strong. This message also shows us that when we become weak from lack of water, we can quickly be revived by drinking water.

We can see in the verses below that water was needed and supplied by God.

Deuteronomy 8:15 (NIV) – (He led you through the great and terrible wilderness, with its fiery serpents and scorpions and thirsty ground where there was no water; He brought water for you out of the rock of flint.)

Psalm 78:15-16 (NKJ) – (He split the rocks in the wilderness and gave them abundant drink like the depths. He also brought streams out of rock and caused waters to run down like rivers.)

Nehemiah 9:15 (NKJ) – (You provided bread from heaven for them for their hunger, you brought forth water from rock for them for their thirst and you told them to enter in order to possess the land which you swore to give them.)

Yes, water is essential for our health and well-being; it is a must for renewing our youth physically, mentally, and spiritually. God has supplied us and continues to supply us with water to sustain us. Let's look at one more verse on what happens when we become dehydrated from insufficient water.

Isaiah 44:12 (NKJ) – (The blacksmith with the tongs works one in the coals, fashions it with hammers and works it with the strength of his arms. Even so, he is hungry, and his strength fails; he drinks no water and is faint.)

As we can see -- even the blacksmith, with his strong arms, becomes weak and faint without enough water. I hope I have convinced you now to stay hydrated and drink enough water to keep up your strength and to stay healthy!

While we could get into great detail on how to stay hydrated and how much water to drink. I feel led to give you an important tip that anyone can follow that will not only help hydrate you but also keep up your body's minerals and electrolytes.

That is taking in a bit of good quality sea salt. Not traditional table salt but sea salt. To simplify this I use Celtic sea salt or Himalayan salt. There is a long list of benefits to consuming a bit of Celtic or Himalayan salt, but below is a short list of known benefits.

1- They are loaded with trace minerals the body needs, but most people are low in these life-sustaining minerals.

2- They prevent dehydration and help you keep up your electrolytes.

3- They promote your brain, muscles, and nervous system function.

4- They support your digestive system and help you absorb key nutrients.

Because of these health-enhancing benefits, you can also notice better quality sleep, better-regulated blood pressure, fewer muscle cramps, better recovery after exercise, and increased physical energy throughout your day.

Over a very short period of time, you will notice a substantial difference in the way you feel. This is largely due to the increases in trace minerals going into your body which helps with the hydration process.

The two simple suggestions I have for taking in the high-quality Celtic or Himalayan salt are these. You can simply sprinkle a little bit on your food just like many do now with traditional table salt. However, if you decide to put the sea salt on your food, I highly suggest not to use any traditional salt anymore but, simply use the high-quality sea salt.

I personally don't use salt on my food. Instead, I put a little in my drinking water, which seems to greatly enhance my hydration and keep my energy at a good level throughout the day. I simply take a little pinch of the salt between my thumb and forefinger and drop it into my bottle of water and give it a shake. I usually add the sea salt to my water a couple of times a day. Although this is a simple tip, it is very helpful for your health and will aid in renewing your youth.

Even though hydrating your body and quenching your thirst is highly important, it can't compare to quenching the thirst of your soul and where you spend eternity.

Psalm 42:1-2 (NKJ) – (As the deer pants for the water brooks, so pants my soul for you, O God. My soul thirsts for God, for the living God.)

This is an extremely powerful verse, and you can see in life that people are looking for satisfaction, and they are thirsty to find their way and what will give them true lasting peace. Jesus is who they are looking for and the only one who can truly satisfy this thirst!

Matthew 5:6 (NKJ) – (Blessed are those who hunger and thirst for righteousness, for they shall be filled.)

As we mentioned in the opening pages of this book, one of the benefits of the followers of Jesus is the renewing of their youth like the eagles. To have this benefit, you must first know Jesus by making him Lord and Savior of your life. If you have done so, that is great, and your renewed youth is your benefit to claim and grasp hold of.

If you have not accepted Jesus into your heart, I highly encourage you to do so right now by admitting you're a sinner, asking Jesus to forgive you of your sins, and invite him into your heart as Lord and Savior and trusting him. As we close this chapter and this book comes to an end, let's look at the verse in John chapter 4 again!

(Whoever drinks of the water that I will give him shall never thirst, but the water that I will give him will become in him a well of water springing up to eternal life.)

# THE FINAL WORD

I feel strongly that the words in this book were divinely given to me by the Holy Spirit of God! I also believe that if you follow these Biblical principles, you will experience a powerful renewing that will start in your spirit and then flow divinely into your mind and physical body, making you feel, look, and act younger and more vibrant! You will become all that God created you to be, and everyone around you will notice this renewing as God satisfies you with long life, length of days and shows you his salvation in Jesus' name! Amen and Amen!

Proverbs 9:11 – (For by me your days will be multiplied and years of life will be added to you.

www.ingramcontent.com/pod-product-compliance
Lightning Source LLC
Chambersburg PA
CBHW071502080526
44587CB00014B/2184